HOMESCHOOLING

A Quick Guide to Online, Homeschooling, and Unschooling

(How to Homeschool Your Children for the Best Education Possible)

Mary McBride

Published by Harry Barnes

Mary McBride

All Rights Reserved

Homeschooling: A Quick Guide to Online, Homeschooling, and Unschooling (How to Homeschool Your Children for the Best Education Possible)

ISBN 978-1-7778032-9-2

All rights reserved. No part of this guide may be reproduced in any form without permission in writing from the publisher except in the case of brief quotations embodied in critical articles or reviews.

Legal & Disclaimer

The information contained in this book is not designed to replace or take the place of any form of medicine or professional medical advice. The information in this book has been provided for educational and entertainment purposes only.

The information contained in this book has been compiled from sources deemed reliable, and it is accurate to the best of the Author's knowledge; however, the Author cannot guarantee its accuracy and validity and cannot be held liable for any errors or omissions. Changes are periodically made to this book. You must consult your doctor or get professional medical advice before using any of the suggested remedies, techniques, or information in this book.

Upon using the information contained in this book, you agree to hold harmless the Author from and against any damages, costs, and expenses, including any legal fees potentially resulting from the application of any of the information provided by this guide. This disclaimer applies to any damages or injury caused by the use and application, whether directly or indirectly, of any advice or information presented, whether for breach of contract, tort, negligence, personal injury, criminal intent, or under any other cause of action.

You agree to accept all risks of using the information presented inside this book. You need to consult a professional medical practitioner in order to ensure you are both able and healthy enough to participate in this program.

Table of Contents

INTRODUCTION 1

CHAPTER 1: WHAT ARE THE REASONS FOR LEARNING AT HOME, INSTEAD OF SCHOOL? 4

CHAPTER 2: DECIDING ON A HOMESCHOOL STYLE 8

CHAPTER 3: HOMESCHOOLING CONCERNS 15

CHAPTER 4: THE COST OF HOMESCHOOLING – FINANCING IT 19

CHAPTER 5: TIMETABLING HINTS 28

CHAPTER 6: HOMESCHOOL NAYSAYERS 34

CHAPTER 7: THE DREADED TRANSCRIPT 40

CHAPTER 8: THE UN-SCHOOLING PROCEDURE 57

CHAPTER 9: HOMESCHOOLING ENABLES YOU TO GIVE YOUR CHILDREN MORE IN-DEPTH ATTENTION AND SUPPORT IN THE SUBJECTS OR ACTIVITIES WITH WHICH THEY STRUGGLE OR EXCEL. 63

CHAPTER 10: LEARNING IN HOMESCHOOLING 65

CHAPTER 11: 10 TIPS FOR TEACHING MATHEMATICH 71

CHAPTER 12: TRADITIONAL APPROACH (ALL-IN-ONE CURRICULA) 82

CHAPTER 13: SELECTING A HOMESCHOOLING CURRICULUM 98

CHAPTER 14: REDUCE COMMITMENTS AWAY FROM HOME 111

CHAPTER 15: SHOULD YOU HOMESCHOOL? 130

CHAPTER 16: THE LEGALITIES 140

CHAPTER 17: SNOW DAYS KEEPING YOUR KIDS ON TASK EVEN DURING SNOW DAYS 147

CHAPTER 18: WHAT IF MY KID WON'T LEARN FROM ME? 157

CHAPTER 19: HOW TO MOTIVATE YOUR HOMESCHOOLED CHILD 174

CHAPTER 20: HOW TO FIND PROGRAMS FOR HOMESCHOOLED KIDS' SOCIAL INTERACTION 181

CONCLUSION 189

Introduction

Homeschooling has now become one of the alternative education models that are in demand by families in various countries. Homeschooling is an educational practice that optimizes the intelligence potential possessed by each individual. According to Bunday, homeschooling is a learning or education system with an at home approach and is popularized as an alternative education at the family level and places children as subjects of learning .

Homeschooling is one of the alternative child-friendly schools in the future. Homeschooling accelerates the achievement of a civilized learning community. The approach model that focuses on multiple intelligences and children's absorption ability is in accordance with the concept of education that prioritizes the humanistic element.

Homeschooling can be stated as an effective alternative education in developing children's potential. The direct output of homeschooling is academic excellence, community builder and good character. Homeschooling or home schooling is an educational model that places the family as the main educator. Homeschooling first developed in the United States in line with the thought of John Caldwell Holt in the 1960s.

Holt's basic thinking is that "humans are basically learning creatures and enjoy learning; we don't need to be shown how to study. The pleasure of learning is killed by people who try to interrupt, regulate, or control it ". Holt's thoughts do not necessarily bring up homeschooling as an alternative education for children, but that thought triggers families and education circles to think critically about education and school. Holt's philosophy related to homeschooling does not only take the view that education is an academic provision for life and not just transferring the school model to the home. Education in homeschooling is seen as a natural experience that befell individuals in their daily lives when these individuals interact with one another.

Chapter 1: What Are The Reasons For Learning At Home, Instead Of School?

Perhaps at first, parents think about withdrawing their children from school when they encounter a problem. Possibly the child is late to develop and still needs individual help. The teacher cannot always be by her side, and therefore the little student is falling further and further behind in her learning until she falls behind the other schoolchildren and thus embarrassed and unmotivated. Or it may be that he is a very advanced child, already understands the subject, and sits idle while the teacher reviews the lesson with the others in the class. Meanwhile, bored as she is, she gets naughty and does something wrong. If I were more intellectually stimulated, I would find no reason for mischief.

Other reasons presented for consideration by those interested in teaching children may include: The opportunity to include a philosophy or belief system in conjunction with other studies; The desire to protect children from drugs, immorality, and even weapons that have appeared in some schools; A need, whether due to illness or allergy, to remove them from the group; Cases of always being on the road (military or missionaries) or engaged in some sport or other talent requiring a lot of focus throughout the year.

There is a more important reason than all the others. These are parents who love their children very much and want to share life with them, including their studies. If I taught them to walk, and they learned with me to talk, to say 'please' and 'thank you', and a thousand other abilities, what reason is there to send them away to learn to read and count? When I already possess such skills and can share them as well.

The purpose is not to compete with schools or to invent a new way of educating children. Instead, we want to return to the initial system when parents had full responsibility for youth education. Those parents who are already dedicated to facilitating the physical, intellectual, and spiritual development of their children will have the best successes in this task, especially when learning to get rid of the school mentality and allow themselves to develop a more natural system.

For those parents who are used to getting rid of their children as soon as possible, sending them to kindergartens and nursery schools, it will be difficult for them to understand what this is about homeschooling. Just as in years past, when mothers were told to give boys bottled milk, in preference to the most natural food for babies, they were wrong. Now we know that not only health but also the affection and the spiritual connection between the mother and the child are affected by the decision regarding the way of feeding them. And so it is also more natural and healthy for children to learn at home and imitate their loved ones.

Chapter 2: Deciding On A Homeschool Style

As a new homeschooling family, you might feel perplexed as to which style of educating to pick. With the many blogs, groups, books, and opinions floating around the homeschool stratosphere, you have a great deal of options to mull over. Keep in mind that how you choose to homeschool is a personal choice and nobody should dictate this decision but you and your children's other parent. You know your kids and their individual learning styles better than anyone else does. With that being said, the most popular homeschooling styles are the controversial unschooling option and of course the traditional method that, mimics the public/private school system in many ways. Some parents opt to mix the two methods and balance them together. In the next few sub-chapters, you will be taking a closer look at the aforementioned methods and what they consist of.

– Traditional Schooling

As you might have already guessed, taking a traditional schooling approach and applying it to your homeschool means that you are opting for a structured way of learning much like the public/private school system has to offer. Many parents feel more comfortable taking this approach as they feel their kids are staying on target with other children their age. If this is your mindset, that is OK, however, you should also know that it is all right to allow your kids to learn at their own pace.

If you opt for traditional schooling, you will want to purchase a curriculum. You will find that there are many to choose from and range in style. We will discuss the various types and a few popular vendors on curriculum programs in the curriculum sub-chapter.

Some families even go as far as purchasing actual desks for their children; however, you can still use a traditional method and educate your kids at the kitchen table with the same results.

Outlining a schedule for how your school day is going to be is a great plan. Since you are taking a more organized approach, plan your entire day out by starting when you wake up in the morning until it is your children's bedtime. Hang the schedule on a corkboard or refrigerator so your kids can easily see it. This will help everyone stay on task. You can make the schedule out day-by-day, week-to-week, or month-to-month.

Remember, even if you opt for traditional homeschooling, you can still put your own personal spin on your program. The greatest thing about home educating is that you always have a choice in how you choose to run your program.

– Unschooling

What do you think of when you hear the word, "unschooling"? Unfortunately, many people associate it with children running wild and lacking educational supervision, however, this simply is not true.

Unschooling is the practice of child-lead learning. What this means is your child learns at his or her own pace by showing interest in various subjects versus having a parent decide what they will be learning for them. For example, instead of learning how to count money at the age of 5 your child might express more of an interest in learning to read first. The theory is that children learn better, when they are actually interested in the subjects they are engaging in.

Some of the apprehension that parents might feel when considering unschooling is that their kids will fall behind their peers, however, if you choose this method you have to train yourself not to care. Many unschooled kids will learn at different rates but the result will always be the same; they will still learn how to read, write, and multiply by the time, they are ready to face the world on their own.

All forms of homeschooling come with some stigma and unwanted criticisms from people who simply do not understand and unschooling seem to receive the most backlash. Train yourself not to care. You know what is best for your kids and if you choose to take an unschooling approach, embrace it with all that you have.

Unschooling is a cheaper way to educate your children as it requires no formal curriculum. You will find that the world is your classroom. In addition to learning basic educational principles, unschooled kids also gain knowledge in many others areas such as gardening, cooking, sewing, volunteering, and even a trade.

– Curriculum

Curriculum consists of a learning program, which typically includes textbooks and other visuals. There is a large variety of companies that manufacture homeschool curriculums and all of them differ in order to fit your family's needs. Some curriculums use faith-based learning materials and incorporate the teachings of the Bible into the studies while others are secular and do not teach religion.

You might opt to choose your curriculum ala cart. A certain company's math studies might catch your eye over another and so on. Most manufacturers allow you to purchase subjects one-by-one for this very reason. You also have the option to buy entire sets. Keep in mind that some websites like www.starfall.com provide free printable and learning resources for your children. The internet is packed with free educational links that you can use to supplement your curriculum with. This helps you save some money in the long run.

Perhaps you wish to engage in a traditional learning program but you are not interested in purchasing a curriculum, which is OK, devise your own. A lot of parents create their own "textbooks" by putting together researched materials that they find on the internet, at the library, and in books. This works particularly well for younger students.

Some popular curriculum vendors include Alpha and Omega, MathUSee, Singapore Math, and Abeka. This list is just a taste of what is out there for you and your children to choose from. Your best bet is to visit homeschool websites, make phone calls to the vendors, ask questions, and do plenty of research to choose a program that works best for you.

Chapter 3: Homeschooling Concerns

Additional Questions and Concerns

You may be considering homeschooling your child if you don't trust the educational system in your area. This is the main reason homeschooling has become more popular around the world. Unanswered questions or concerns shouldn't make you feel defeated. These are some of the most common questions regarding homeschooling.

Is Homeschooling Legal?

It is legal in most countries to educate your children at home. You can find out the laws in your area if you are unsure. Some countries require that parents have at least a bachelor's degree, while others require that they have a diploma in education. These details can be found on the official website of your country's department of education. For a more detailed explanation, you can visit a local office.

Can I home-school my child even if I am not a teacher?

It is not true that licensed teachers offer the best education for children. As a parent, you can do more for your child by building a relationship with them. Parents of homeschooled kids are often those who have no teaching experience or profession.

Do I risk my child being left behind by academically-skilled peers?

Research shows that children who are home-schooled have an average of a year more academic achievement than their school-educated peers. Children who are home-schooled have been shown to communicate more effectively. They also have deeper thinking and are more confident in their studies. They are not academically or socially challenged in any way.

When should I start homeschooling my child?

Because your child has been learning from you since birth, there is no way to know when homeschooling should begin. You can begin teaching your child when your child reaches 5 years old, if you're concerned about that specific year. This is the age at which your child should start school. It's the same age most parents send their kids to pre-school. Your child can be sent to preschool, school, or home school. You can decide what you want, but it is best to start when both of you are ready.

What is the Cost of Homeschooling?

It all depends on you. Online resources can be used to help you build your curriculum if you don't want homeschooling to be expensive. The good news is that almost all educational resources are easily accessible online, making homeschooling an affordable option. If you are looking for the best education for your child, you can buy educational toys and other books. You will discover that your expenses will be lower than when you send your child off to school.

Homeschooling Your Child Early and Taking Your Child out of School

There is a big difference between homeschooling your child young and sending him to school. First, your child will miss his school friends and feel isolated if he has been to school. However, if your child was home-schooled from the beginning, he may not know much about school and might envy his neighbors. Whatever the reason, you should be ready to answer questions such as "Why are they homeschooling?" Be as specific and truthful as possible. Your child may choose to attend school. This is a legal and natural obligation.

Chapter 4: The Cost Of Homeschooling – Financing It

We glanced at this subject earlier, and yes at first sight, homeschooling might look as a cheaper option. However, every individual family's situation is different. You might have no idea how you will do without a second income or job. Again there is options. Budget, make the sums. You will save on stuff like school fees, fuel and so forth. On the other hand it might increase your electricity bill, food bill, and the costs for setting up a learning room might be a large initial sum.

My advice is get creative. Do your homework, get the best deals you can and even try starting a little home-based business with your children. This was something we did successfully. It helped with the finances and also taught my children entrepreneurial skills from a young age that they would have never been able to learn anywhere else.

Cost and finances, especially in today's time and age is a serious consideration. I urge you to do every single sum you possibly can, even if it means saving up first before you start.

But do not let finances alter your dream and vision. Trust me you can do this with little, and slowly progress. At the end of the day all you need is a will to teach and willing minds to learn.

Proponents against homeschooling will use this as their secret weapon. They will discourage you to abandon the process and idea. Always remember you are the only one that knows your own financial situation. Do your sums, and make up your mind. Believe me, where there is a will...there is a way.

We started with nothing. Started a home based business first and the moment that business started to hit half my old salary we did started homeschooling. It is up to you.

Again, here is the perfect place to get support from your support group. Most people started at the exact same point as you. They might even have text books, equipment and so forth you can get for free or at a very low price.

I know this is repetitive, but it is one of the main reasons people abandon the dream. Do your homework.

Becoming the home school teacher

Nothing is more important in the equation than the teacher. In most cased the teacher is the parent, a close relative and if in rare instances the finances allow, a paid professional.

Please remember one of the main reasons you decided to take your kids out of the formal schooling environment are for them to experience another learning environment. One of flexibility, fun and creativity. We want the best for our kids. Then give them the best. And the best you can give them is to not be like a normal school teacher. To not conform to only the presentation of facts. Learning needs to be integrated, lovingly, with all its modern flavors for it to interest and benefit your child.

I am going to repeat that statement. It is the foundation of homeschooling and I urge you to read and meditate about it for a while.

Learning needs to be integrated, lovingly, with all its modern flavors for it to interest and benefit your child.

Only parents or grandparents (close relative) in a proper scheduled homeschooling system has the ability to do this.

Do you maybe feel inadequate and lack the confidence to teach? Well, this is again a very common hurdle and as always one that can easily be overcome. In fact, it was one of my biggest fears. Honest, I was lying awake countless nights wondering if I was capable of doing it. Worst, I had so much self-doubt. Was I screwing up my children's future?

Relax, take a breath, visit you support group. There are countless of online resources. And if there are subjects you are feeling inadequate in, do some self-study and courses or hire a tutor. Alternatively, there are Professional curriculum packages, support groups, online help desks, virtual schools and library resources.

When you start out, you may want to make use of the commercial curriculum packages. Readymade software also allows you to record and log important achievements.

At the end of the day, it is a process. And soon you will be able to handle the stress and every single curve ball that can be thrown at you. Do not give up. There is help. All you need to do is determine your own shortcomings and then make a plan how to address them.

How to structure your school year

You have done the schedule. Maybe you have some troubling questions? Should you study continuously, follow the normal public school year plan? Do you include short breaks, vacation? Is there some flexibility in your plan for burn-out breaks? Public holidays?

It sounds daunting...

But like always remember the main attribute of homeschooling...

Flexibility.

You can decide what suits your child's and your needs. You do not have a set pattern to follow. You can schedule your own times, ideas, weeks and months.

Although we always advocate first time homeschoolers to schedule, some parents manage to do without it. Very successfully I might add. For some practiced homeschoolers even changing a curriculum possible. This is mainly possible since lessons are on a day to day basis. Usually this is done through proper goal setting between parent and child, and also more feasible for older children. Again it is up to you, and you know your limitations and your child's capabilities better than anyone else.

It sounds too good to be true, I know. However, we urge beginners to rather start of charting the first few months. Or, better yet, chart and schedule your first year.

We have covered this, but the start of planning is to first identify, what method of homeschooling will you follow, what curriculum, what is the learning preference of your child, what is the work and play schedules and what are your vacation plans. Also include ad-hoc or contingency time for possible burnout as we discussed earlier. Planning for this now has vast physiological value since you know this might happen and you are prepared for it.

Once you have done this, it is time to plan. Write it on a calendar. Work with your child. You both might look at it from the normal school perceptive at the beginning. Using the public schooling calendar has its benefits, especially if your child came from it. It will keep things familiar until your child adapts to the new found flexibility of home schooling. Longer summer breaks allows your child to be in tune with some of their non-homeschooling friends. So talk it over and make a decision together.

Of course there are huge advantages of taking smaller breaks during the year. We discussed burnout earlier and this also gives you the time to be a parent again. It prevent boredom and give opportunities to explore new interests. These breaks can also be educational holidays. If you have the finances take your children on extended field trips. Let them explore other places, cultures and ways of living.

You are in charge. You and your children can decide your school year together. Make this an annual activity and make it a fun activity. It is a perfect time to add the necessary goals and accountability statements.

Chapter 5: Timetabling Hints

If you look at the number of hours we 'school' our students here in Australia compared to, for example, Finland, we frankly 'over-school' our kids – with very little gain, I believe. In Finland, children in the early years school finish at lunchtime, they have no homework in the elementary years and minimal homework in high school. The Finns' ethos is 'less is best'. Additionally, in the PISA test – Program for International Student Assessment – conducted internationally, their students perform way better than Australian students do for example. In the period 2015–2016, the average score of PISA Maths, English and Science saw Finland rank 8th and Australia rank 21st.[2] There are many other factors that make Finland a successful education system and some that we could quite easily adopt here in Australia. These include no homework, more breaks, more unstructured play, more Music and Art and having the same teacher for a minimum of three years. Finland's approach to education is well worth looking into online, at your convenience. So, when timetabling, think of **quality** of hours rather that **quantity** of hours. I would suggest for road-schoolers and home schoolers aged 8 upwards, around three hours in the morning, Monday to Friday. That then gives you and your child/children the rest of the day to do real-life exploring and adventuring. One of the great things about road schooling and being on the move is the rich experiences your child/children derive from visiting different places. They will likely be learning some history and science through your travels and often the first-hand experience they get will compensate or, in some cases, even go beyond what they'd learn in a conventional school.

If you think you and your child/children can manage more work on any given day, then do so. You may not do as much the next day. And in many cases, there will be opportunities for informally consolidating the morning's learning that has taken place. Children are freshest and energised in the mornings so this is the best time for formal learning. In some schooling situations, I've witnessed students working all day and/or in the evening to get their workload completed. How exhausting and disengaging. Is it any wonder students can become non-compliant and rebellious? Leave it for the next day if it hasn't been possible to complete in 'school' that day – it's not worth the bunfight.

To prepare, write your daily timetable up on a large piece of paper board and make it colourful and clear for all to follow. Display for all to see in an accessible position. If you have littlies who are yet to read, use visuals, pictures etc. to inform them what is to come. Children, as do adults, function better when they know the plan for the day. It's about making sure that their school day is as predictable as possible.

To prepare for maximum learning, schedule a fitness activity first thing in the morning to get the blood flowing and the brain pumping. A run on the beach or, if you have bikes, a bike ride or encourage you students to set up an obstacle course! Kids are very creative and resourceful when it comes to this.

A musical activity/game is also a great way to start the day. For you, I have written and performed 35 musical activities which are on my website SmarterHappierKids.com

These can be used anytime, anywhere. The videos are based on 'authentic teaching' where I am teaching directly to the children, so you can just sit back and relax. They are lots of fun and very engaging and suitable for early years and primary school children. Unstructured play is another great way to start the day because so much learning is taking place when children are engaged in this form of play. For focusing, kid's yoga activities are excellent. There are plenty of ideas online for this as well.

Another tip for more effective learning. Be mindful to use the 'Breathing in' and 'Breathing out' principle by having an inward type activity (breathing in) such as maths followed by an outward type activity (breathing out) such as running or riding a bike, or a musical, singing activity. Although it's up to you to schedule what and when, I suggest you review and evaluate the timetable at the end of each term. Changes may need to be made as you and your children's needs change.

At the end of your school day, please don't fall into the trap of thinking that you have to set homework. To my way of thinking, homework only robs a child of their freedom and their time to pursue the things they love! There is increasing research and evidence to suggest how ineffective homework is – especially in the formative years. Again, Finland has a no Homework Policy in the younger years and very limited in the senior years, yet learning and wellbeing outcomes are one of the highest in the world! (Refer to P.I.S.A results, O.E.C.D.) Just let your kids play...

Chapter 6: Homeschool Naysayers

Everyone who decides to homeschool their children will run into at least one person, maybe more, that tell them they shouldn't homeschool. The decision to homeschool isn't an easy one to make, and often isn't popular. However, the choice in how your child is educated is entirely up to you, so you need to decide ahead of time how you will deal with the homeschooling naysayers.

One of the quintessential arguments of a homeschooling naysayer is that you're not qualified to teach your own child, regardless if you have a Bachelor of Arts in Education or not. This argument is ridiculous! If you're a parent, you've already been teaching your child since birth. Who was it that taught your child to talk, walk, and use the restroom by themselves? It was you and your spouse, of course. So, if you could teach them those skills, why wouldn't you be qualified to teach them how to read or do math?

Besides being "unqualified," other naysayers will tell you that teaching a child is too difficult. A public school teacher's job is difficult because he or she has to teach 30 or more children several subjects all in one day. Teaching one, two, or even three children at home is not nearly as difficult as a public school teacher's job.

Another argument you might hear if you're trying to decide if you want to homeschool is that children need socialization. I will discuss the response to this argument in greater detail later in this introduction, where I will offer great opportunities for meaningful socialization for your homeschooled child.

Different Ways to Homeschool

You've done it! You've made the choice to homeschool your children. But now what?

There are several different methods of homeschooling but traditional homeschooling and unschooling are the two most common methods.

Traditional homeschooling is basically concerned with your child learning what is normally taught in public schools. So if you want your children to learn from a pre-planned curriculum which is similar to the curriculum at the public schools, a traditional homeschooling approach would be best for you.

Unschooling is a different approach which has the advantage of giving you much more flexibility as to what subjects you want to teach your child. This approach is also known as "child-led" learning since many parents who choose to use this method will concentrate on teaching their child subjects that the child has more of an interest in. Parents who use the unschooling approach often believe that their children will learn best in a flexible and non-structured environment.

What if I Didn't Do Well in School?

If you are considering homeschooling your children, you might be apprehensive if you didn't do well in school yourself. Thankfully your success, or lack thereof, in school does not have to be an issue in choosing to homeschool. In fact, you can take advantage of the time you're teaching your child to brush up on some of the things you didn't do so well with when you were in school.

Math is one subject that parents stress over when they choose to homeschool, especially if they struggled when they went to school. Your struggles shouldn't be a factor in choosing to homeschool. If you weren't good in math, remember you'll have the teacher's manual with the answers. However, you may have to spend a little bit of time relearning, or learning anew, the concepts prior to trying to teach your child. And remember, you can always turn to other homeschooling families to help you if you need it.

Science is another subject that parents worry about teaching because they don't feel qualified to teach it. However, there are a number of good science curriculums available, and some of them include all of the materials for experiments. You were probably turned off by smelling formaldehyde when you dissected a frog in biology class but your kids can dissect a virtual frog right on the internet!

Reading should be one of the easiest subjects to teach. Your children will learn to love reading if they see you and your spouse read, no matter what the book is. Read books aloud with your child and then have them re-tell you the story in their own words. If they are just learning how to read, one resource that is popular with homeschoolers is "Teach Your Child to Read in 100 Easy Lessons" by Siegfried Englemann, Phyllis Haddox, and Elaine Bruner.

Homeschool Consultants will assist you with making curriculum choices and selecting the best materials for a small consulting fee.

Chapter 7: The Dreaded Transcript

Your child's high school transcript is probably the most important piece of paper you will produce during her academic career. It sums up all four years of her education and will be scrutinized by college admissions officers and scholarship critics alike.

I know it seems daunting at first – especially since it has to both read impressively and look professional – but it really shouldn't be too hard. As long as you've been good about keeping a record of your child's grades, all you really have to worry about is organizing everything into a single easy-to-read document.

Here's how my mom did it.

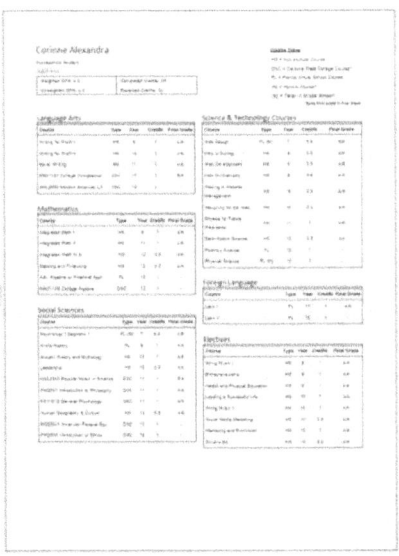

As you can see, it is important to include a number of things:

- The child's first and last name

- The fact that the child was homeschooled, and the homeschool address (your home)

- All courses taken during high school (organized by subject or grade)

- Types of curriculum (i.e. home, online, dual enrollment)

- The year each course was taken

- Credits earned

- Final Grades (some are missing from my transcript because I was still in the process of taking those classes when applying to colleges)

- GPA (you can follow our example below or use one of the many free GPA calculators online)

That's all there is to it. Again, you don't need a super fancy document. Keep it well-organized, and easy to read – it's the classes and grades themselves that should wow admissions officers.

If you're unsure about how to apply credits or want to calculate your child's GPA manually, my mom (being the amazing person that she is) organized the following guide just for you!

HOW TO APPLY CREDITS:

140-180 hours of study and schoolwork (usually completed over an 8-9 month period) = 1 credit

1 college class (usually completed over a 3-4 month period) = 1 credit

70-90 hours of study and schoolwork (usually completed over a 3-4 month period) = ½ credit

35 to 45 hours of study and schoolwork (usually completed over a 6-8 week period) = ¼ credit

HOW WE CALCULATED MY GPA:

1. We assigned point values to each letter grade. For college and honors courses, we added 1 point to the final grade. We also added 1 point to high school courses I took from Florida Virtual while I was still in "middle school."

90-100% = A = 4 points

80-89% = B = 3 points

70-79% = C = 2 points

60-69% = D = 1 point

< 60% = F = 0 points

2) We calculated the total points I earned by multiplying the point value times the credit value.

For example, I took seven 1 credit Social Science courses and three 0.5 credit courses. I earned an A in all of them. Five of the one credit courses were college courses, and one of the half credit courses was a Florida Virtual high school course I took while still in "middle school." For the college courses and the course I took in middle school, we added one point to the final grade. So I earned a total of 39.5 points from my Social Science classes.

FLVS Psychology – 0.5 credit x 5 points = 2.5 points earned

World History – 1 credit x 4 points = 4 points earned

Ancient History & Mythology – 1 credit x 4 points = 4 points earned

Leadership – 0.5 credit x 4 points = 2 points earned

Popular Music (college) – 1 credit x 5 points = 5 points earned

Philosophy (college) – 1 credit x 5 points = 5 points earned

Psychology (college) – 1 credit x 5 points = 5 points earned

Geography – 0.5 credit x 4 points = 2 points earned

Government (college) - 1 credit x 5 points = 5 points earned

Ethics (college) – 1 credit x 5 points = 5 points earned

Total Points from Social Science : 39.5

In addition to the 39.5 points I earned from my social science courses, I earned 22 points from my English courses, 19 points from my math courses, 30 points from my science and technology courses, 8 points from my foreign language courses, and 28 points from my electives.

Total from all courses: 39.5 + 22 + 19 + 30 + 8 + 28 = 146.5 total points

3) We calculated my total credits. I had a total of 34 credits between 27 one credit courses and 14 half credit courses.

4) Then to calculate the grade point average you take the total points and divide them by the total credits.

146.5 / 34 = 4.3 GPA

Depending on the type of college (if any) you are planning on attending, you should aim for 6-8 credits per year. Visit the admissions section of the websites of the colleges you are wanting to attend and check to see what courses they are expecting applicants to have taken.

For example, Georgia Tech requires all applicants to have taken the following courses:

- English - 4 Units
- Math - 4 Units
- Science - 4 Units
- Social Science - 3 Units
- Foreign Language - 2 Units (of the same language)

In addition, for homeschool students, they ask for "supplementary information to demonstrate academic ability in core academic areas. " The core academic areas they are describing are the areas listed above. They prefer for the demonstration of ability to be in the form of SAT Subject tests, AP/IB scores, and/or previous college coursework.

These requirements are common for most colleges. This is why I made sure to demonstrate my abilities in each of the core academic areas with at least two classes. Here's how I did it, how my younger sister who just finished up her junior year of high school is doing it, and suggestions for how you might accomplish it.

English*

What I did:

For English I took two courses at my local community college: College Composition and Modern American Literature.

What my sister is doing:

She has taken two English classes offered by Florida Virtual and will take College Composition at our local community college next year.

What you could do:

- SAT Literature Subject Test
- AP English Language and Composition
- AP English Literature and Composition

- English courses available at a local college

- English courses available from an online public school

Math*

What I did:

For math, I took Advanced Algebra with Financial Applications through the online public school Florida Virtual, and I took College Algebra through the local community college.

What my sister is doing:

She is taking Pre-Calculaus through Florida Virtual and will take a math class at our local community college next year.

What you could do:

- SAT Mathematics Level I Subject Test

- SAT Mathematics Level II Subject Test

- AP Calculus AB
- AP Calculus BC
- AP Statistics
- Math courses available at a local college
- Math courses available from an online public school

Science

What I did:

To demonstrate my abilities in science, I took Forensic Science and Honors Physical Science through Florida Virtual.

What my sister is doing:

She took Honors Physical Science through Florida Virtual and will take Honors Physics through Florida Virtual next year.

What you could do:

- SAT Biology Subject Test

- SAT Chemistry Subject Test
- SAT Physics Subject Test
- AP Biology
- AP Chemistry
- AP Environmental Science
- AP Physics C: Electricity and Magnetism
- AP Physics C: Mechanics
- AP Physics 1: Algebra-Based
- AP Physics 2: Algebra-Based
- Lab Science courses available at a local college
- Lab Science courses available from an online public school

Social Sciences

What I did:

For the social sciences, I took five courses at my local community college. These included Philosophy, Popular Music in

America, Psychology, American Government, and Ethics.

What my sister is doing:

She took Honors Physical Science through Florida Virtual and will take Honors Physics through Florida Virtual next year.

What you could do:

- SAT U.S. History Subject Test
- SAT World History Subject Test
- AP Comparative Government and Politics
- AP European History
- AP Human Geography
- AP Macroeconomics
- AP Microeconomics
- AP Psychology
- AP United States Government and Politics

- AP United States History
- AP World History
- History, civics/government, psychology and/or philosophy courses available at a local college
- History, civics/government, psychology and/or philosophy available from an online public school
-

Foreign Language:

What I did:

I'm fascinated by Ancient Greece and Greek philosophy, so while I would have preferred to learn Greek, I ended up studying Latin I and Latin II through Florida Virtual. I could have studied Greek on my own, but I wouldn't have been able to demonstrate my abilites to a college, and I simply didn't have time to study two languages. On a positive note, I am taking Ancient Greek at Rollins with a fantastic professor who also teaches Greek philosophy, and I have found my experience with Latin to be useful in learning Ancient Greek.

What my sister is doing:

My sister took Latin I through Florida Virtual. Classes at Florida Virtual can sometimes be great and sometimes not be so great. Latin on Florida Virtual is one of those that is not so great. The Latin teachers are wonderful, but the course itself is difficult to learn from. Because of this, my sister decided to not take Latin II through Florida Virtual, but instead take Italian at the local high school. One of the great things about Florida, is that students may take up to 3 classes a year at their local high school and do the rest of their classes as a homeschooler. Since she needs two years of the same foreign language, she will be taking Italian at the local community college next year.

What you could do:

- SAT Subject Tests are available for Spanish, Latin, German Japanese, French, Chinese (Mandarin), Italian, and Korean
- AP Chinese Language and Culture
- AP French Language and Culture
- AP German Language and Culture
- AP Italian Language and Culture
- AP Japanese Language and Culture
- AP Latin
- AP Spanish Language and Culture
- AP Spanish Literature and Culture
- Foreign language courses available at a local college
- Foreign language courses available from an online public school

*Note about English and Math: You would think that a good score on math and English portions of the regular SAT would count for demonstrating your ability, but most colleges are looking for more than that.

Chapter 8: The Un-Schooling Procedure

Un-schooling is also referred to as the interest-led and natural approach because it lets your child lead the learning process by allowing him/her to learn from routine life experience and does not use any formal lessons or school schedules to teach.

In un-schooling, your child has complete liberty to follow his/her interests and learn in almost the same way an adult does by following his/her curiosity or interest. The same way children learn how to talk, walk, and express their feelings is the same way unschooled kids learn how to read, write, complete math problems, and so on.

Pros and Cons of the Un-schooling Approach

This is a great approach for you and your kids if you do not wish to use any pre-packaged material and if you want your child to have complete control over his or her learning.

In this homeschooling approach, you occasionally provide your child with different experiences but mostly let him/her learn from everyday life experiences and improve his/her knowledge and understanding of the world around him or her as well as of different subjects.

For instance, if your child likes to explore, you let him/her do that by providing him/her different materials to explore and understand. If your child enjoys playing at the swings, you take him/her to a local park and let him/her play around, fall, and get back up on his/her own to teach him or her the way to care for himself/herself.

One of the biggest advantages of this approach is that it provides your child with the time, freedom, and research abilities to become an expert in his/her area of interest. Additionally, you do not enforce anything on him/her; you let your child learn at his/her own pace without forcing lessons on him/her.

While this approach is quite popular among parents who like to give their kids freedom to learn things, your child may lag behind a little or more on grade level assessments. For instance, your 7-year-old child may have learned a lot about digestion or plants as compared to a 10 year old, but may not know how to read properly. This can present difficulties for your child if you wish to put him back into the school system at some point.

However, if you are not too concerned with whether your child does well at grade level assignments and wish to give your child the freedom he/she needs to explore and understand the world on his/her own, this approach is quite suitable for you. Additionally, if your child does not like "being pushed" towards things and instead enjoys learning without a set schedule, this method will suit him/her well.

Below is an example of a typical un-schooling schedule:

A Typical Unschooling Schedule

Every un-schooler is different; therefore, if you opt to use this approach, you need to focus on your child's interests and his/her routine. With that said, a typical un-schooling schedule looks more or less like this.

Your child wakes up when he/she feels well rested and after, you let the child decide what he/she would like to do that day. You can give your child a list of activities and chores to do and ask for input on what he or she would like to do. Mostly, unschooled kids set goals for themselves with the guidance of parents and work with them to create an effective schedule that helps them fulfill their goals. Every day will be different and on each day, the child will learn something different. However, if your child wants, he/she can repeat one or two activities on several days to get better at it.

You can leave different tools, equipment, books, and apparatus on the table or in the child's room for exploration. However, make sure you are nearby when what you leave in the room is something dangerous or harmful such as a glass chemistry set.

Mostly, un-schoolers spend the afternoon or evening in the community engaging in volunteer work, a part-time job, studying at the library, or doing anything else that helps them pursue their passions.

Focus on what your child enjoys most and provide resources and materials related to it. If your child likes to learn about dinosaurs, provide more books and documentaries on the topic. If your child is a math whiz, help him/her learn more math related stuff.

The Charlotte Mason approach is another homeschooling method very similar to the un-schooling approach. The next section highlights it in detail.

Chapter 9: Homeschooling Enables You To Give Your Children More In-Depth Attention And Support In The Subjects Or Activities With Which They Struggle Or Excel.

Those who choose to homeschool have a great opportunity to give their children the individualized attention that they need as they are learning. They are able to notice which subjects or extracurricular activities their children have difficulty with and are thus able to give sufficient time and effort to helping their children work through their problems with these subjects or activities.

Homeschoolers who customize their own curriculum have the advantage of accelerating learning in the areas where students excel. For example, a child may excel in science but struggle with math. In this case, the child may be advancing at an 8th grade level in science while staying on target at 6th grade math. In a conventional school, the teacher's task is to get the students through the grade. This objective is what the teacher bases his or her instruction on. It doesn't really matter whether some students in the class are way ahead in some subjects or if some students are lagging in other subjects. In this set-up, there is a risk of students getting through the grade without really mastering skills necessary for the next grade. In homeschooling, students get the individualized instruction and attention that they need to master the skills required before they can move on to the next skill level.

Chapter 10: Learning In Homeschooling

It is essential to understand the learning process before teaching can occur. Even the smallest details can help parents to understand how to share knowledge with students who are difficult. Teachers all over the globe use a variety of theories to teach their students. This is only a small selection, but the ones that are most popular with educators are included.

Simply put, learning refers to "the acquisition of new or modified behavior, knowledge, and values through various modes of information acquisition and/or synthesis." Humans, animals, and some machines all have the ability to learn. It is inaccurate to say that learning is simply the acquisition of or collection information. Learning is building on what is already known. Without a foundation, learning cannot be achieved. It is possible to argue that no new information can be extracted from newly acquired skills. Although it can occur involuntarily, or unconsciously, it is not mandatory.

Learning curve is an essential term in education and academic circles. It refers to the accumulation of all necessary information over time in order for the creation of new, coherent and useful knowledge. It is essential to understand the concept of learning curves when teaching any subject or skill.

It is helpful to understand the basics of how to give new information to someone in education, whether you are homeschooling or general education.

Habituation is a form of non-associative learning in psychology. This refers to a decrease in response probability due to repeated stimuli. This means that the probability of a random response is significantly reduced when stimuli are repeatedly repeated.

Sensitization is another non-associative form of learning. It involves the amplifying of a response to a repeated stimulus.

Associative learning refers to the process of learning an association between two stimuli, behavior, or stimulus. There are two types of associative learning.

Operant and classical conditioning

Other theories include Imprinting, Observational learning, and Enculturation. However, this is only a small part of the main topic, which is homeschooling. The Theory of Multiple Intelligences, Episodic Learning and Multimedia Learning are all more relevant to homeschooling.

According to psychologists, there is three types of learning. They are Cognitive, Psychomotor, and Affective. This applies to homeschooling as understanding the three domains can help you understand how to respond to the teaching methods used. Cognitive and psychomotor development will be predominant in the early years of learning. However, as they age, affective learning will be essential.

It is easy to say that learning at first is similar to painting on a large, blank canvas. As you add color, a better picture will form as a component of larger scenery. Start with the primary colors, and then mix them together to create secondary hues. Start with stick figures, then move on to more complex two-dimensional representations until you are able to create three-dimensional models. Although this might seem a bit simplistic, you will get the idea.

Homeschooling is a way to learn and understand. Although there may be some concepts that are difficult to explain or explain (e.g., why 1 plus 1 equals 2), they are meant to be accepted as theorems. However, there are many ideas that can be used to help your child understand.

Collaborative learning is another option that might be of use to you. It includes several stages of learning from the youngest (according their conceptual framework) to oldest presumed age of learners.

Learning Style Discovery Stage

The Exploration Stage

The Collaborative Learning Stage

The Gift Focus Stage

The Transitional Stage

Here are some memorable quotes about learning to close out this chapter.

"I believe that no matter what fortune comes our way, we can give it meaning and make it valuable." --Hermann Hesse, Siddhartha

"(Joan 1941) She wrote me an email asking how I could read it. It's so difficult. It's so hard. I advised her to start from the beginning and go as far as possible until you get lost. Continue reading until you understand the entire book. That's exactly what she did. --Richard P. Feynman

Chapter 11: 10 Tips For Teaching Mathematich

People have emotional responses to the word "Mathematics." Some love it, others hate it. Very few people are neutral towards this topic.

This should signal to any homeschooling parent that their child's attitude is actually more important than his math skills.

If your child has had time to develop a dislike for math, I would say you will have to spend some time with Fred. I am referring to the main character in Life of Fred, a math curriculum which reads like a book full of adventures.

This series will help your child see math with different eyes. Your first grader will understand math is all around, it is needed everyday, and one must learn it in order to make life easier.

Doing mental calculations is the ultimate goal in teaching arithmetic. Reaching for the calculator should only happen if you are adding exceedingly long numbers, doing complicated operations, you are pressed for time, or you are checking your work.

Here are 10 tips for teaching mathematics to your first grader:

1. Choose curriculum carefully.

Learn about different math curricula from Cathy Duffy's website or book on top curriculum picks. Rainbow Resource Center also features good descriptions for the curricula they sell. On HomeschoolWays.com, I have reviewed several math programs: Rod and Staff, Singapore Math, and Right Start Mathematics. Just go to HomeschoolWays.com/reviews for details. It might help to know how each of these is used on a daily basis. There are so many approaches to math these days: spiral versus blocked, Montessori versus traditional etc.

Behind every curriculum, there is a philosophy of education. Do some research by reading the covers, front matter, and introductory chapters in textbooks. Watch how to videos on their websites, if available. Do the hard work now and you will minimize your grief in the long run.

2. Get help from manipulatives.

Abstract ideas must be grasped visually and in a tactile fashion by seven-year-old children. That's where manipulatives come in. Some math programs come with lots of manipulatives, like Right Start, Math-U-See, Abeka and even Saxon. Others will give you ideas as what to buy. Personally, I like to just open the book and know that everything I need is in my math box, ready to go. So I prefer a math curriculum which comes with a book and a manipulative set, but you may be different. Either way, use manipulatives in your math class to help your first grader get math concepts.

3. Don't be afraid to supplement.

We use Right Start Math and we like it. Now and then, if I think my son needs more practice in a certain area, we supplement with Math Mammoth. Right Start staff will tell you that math games provide the practice. Sure, but not for every skill in the book. In first grade, the Corners games give us addition practice, but not for every possible combination of numbers. So we will add a few chapters from Math Mammoth here and there.

There are many websites which will provide math worksheets for free. Be very specific in your search, otherwise you will get lost in the sea of Common Core standards and offerings available.

4. Keep on keeping on.

In Right Start Math, my son likes the math games the most, of course. He dislikes the abacus. And yet, after he sees a new concept is hard to grasp in his mind, he will reluctantly pick up the abacus, work the problem with it, and then notate the results in his math journal.

It's not smooth sailing. Don't expect it to be. But it's a lot more efficient than being in a classroom where a lot of artificial teaching goes on and your child is only one of 20 pupils.

If you persevere, you will see results. Having said that, don't frustrate your child to the point of tears. Please don't misunderstand. Perseverance pays off, but not if your child is crying. If you sense tears are on the horizon, pull back and maybe don't do math for that day. If it's just a matter of your child's immaturity, deal with him gently and show him the algorithm again until he gets it.

5. Be patient.

This goes without saying, but I find that all of us need to be reminded at times. This homeschooling mom told me that she did not know how angry she was inside until she started homeschooling her children. Being angry at your children because of immature things they do is not very mature of an adult.

I recommend you read some books or go to counseling to solve inner wounds you might be carrying, which prevent you from giving your child a nurturing atmosphere. I like John Bradshaw's book, Homecoming: Reclaiming and Championing Your Inner Child. There's no telling how much sadness and grief you are carrying because of your own childhood. Get some help before you mess up your child and continue the vicious cycle.

6. Be gentle.

Charlotte Mason coined the term "the gentle art of teaching." It is a reminder to all of us that we do not want to bring our children to the point of tears. If you feel frustrated or if you see frustration building up in your child, stop teaching math for the day. Just tell your child you two will take a break for today and will resume tomorrow.

If you have been harsh to your child, apologize. Give him a hug. Ask for forgiveness. Children are very sweet and ready to forgive their parents. This humble attitude on your part will work wonders for your relationship and it will teach your child to do the same when he grows up and becomes a parent. We are all in need of grace and cultivating gentleness is part of an ongoing process. You will probably have to apologize many times to your child. That's OK. This is how character is developed. Somebody once said, "There is a high price for a low living." The more you have to apologize, the more you will remember next time before getting harsh. And you will continue to grow.

7. Calculate your work load.

Some of us live in areas where a homeschooled child must be tested once a year. Get those dates early on and put them on your academic calendar. Organize your curriculum around those dates.

In every family there are unexpected events which will stop regularly scheduled activities and turn the academic calendar on its head. Allow yourself a week for those unforeseen events.

Then schedule in regular breaks for sanity. Some people like Sabbath schooling: teaching for six weeks and taking a week off.

The other thing to consider are family trips and big holidays like Thanksgiving, Christmas, birthdays, or a new baby joining the family.

All these elements will help you break down your math book into exactly the kind of increments you need to reach test day prepared.

Planning takes the panic out of teaching. It's a lot easier for me to think I have two pages to teach today than to think I have to teach 150 pages between now and March. Divide and conquer. It worked for the Romans and it works today for homeschool educators.

8. Do math throughout the day.

Cooking, baking, LEGO building, ordering, gardening and many other things we do around the house need mathematical concepts in order to get done. Point this out to your child casually. Solve the math problems together. It will help your child understand how math is part of our every day life and not some abstract concept his parents decided to torture him with in the morning, during school time. Life of Fred, a literature-based math curriculum, helps with this point, too. We read Fred books in the evening during our reading time and we do the exercises orally most of the time.

9. Start teaching money concepts.

Allowance should be used for addition, subtraction and other mathematical operations. We give our children a weekly allowance based on their ages. My first grader, for instance, would receive $7 while he was seven and $8 after he turned 8. That may seem like a lot of money and it is, but the lessons that come with it are priceless. In other words, it is a good investment.

I gave each child three jars. We labeled them Spending, Saving, Giving. First off, we teach them about tithing. That's giving 10% of your earnings to God. This money goes into the Giving jar. They can take their tithe to church or give it to a charitable, non-profit organization dedicated to spreading the gospel. Then, we teach them to put some of their money in the Saving jar. The rest of the money goes into the Spending jar.

Children, like adults, are very interested in money. In the beginning, money means toys. With time and a bit of education, their ideas start changing. In the process, they will have practiced math operations.

10. Sow the seeds of entrepreneurship.

Your seven-year-old first grader might be too young to start his own cottage business, but then again, he might not. You be the judge. At the very least, you can sow the seeds of entrepreneurship with him by giving him a scenario about a lemonade stand, or baking waffles for friends and neighbors, or mowing the lawn or blowing leaves for others.

Show him on paper the potential for earning and what he might need to pay for supplies. Inspiration comes in different forms. Children get motivated by money just as much as adults do, especially once they realize that every LEGO set or special soccer ball they want costs money.

Chapter 12: Traditional Approach (All-In-One Curricula)

The traditional approach (also called all-in-one or structured approach) is the textbook/workbook method that focuses on reading, grammar, writing and spelling. This approach is similar to the teaching curriculum used in public and private schools; sometimes the same textbooks are also used. The traditional curriculum is ready-to-use, detailed, extensive and requires little to no preparation on the part of the parent or tutor. Sometimes tests are also included and the programs let students obtain high school diploma accreditation. It is also one of the most expensive homeschooling curricula. The traditional approach lets a student transition easily from a home learning environment to a traditional school system.

Pros:

1. Detailed
2. Extensive
3. Step-by-step curriculum
4. Allows students to transition easily to a public or private school system
5. Accreditation available

Cons:

1. Expensive
2. Nearly identical to a public or private school curriculum
3. Hard to customize or modify

Classical

The Classical approach to homeschooling follows the "Trivium," a medieval learning method divided into stages. Students start learning fundamental facts and skills and progress to logic and advanced language. In the initial Grammar Stage, they learn about the world. In the Dialectic Stage, they expand on what they learned, compare and contrast, explain why and how and connect reality with abstraction. They learn how to apply their knowledge during the Rhetoric Stage. The last stage, Logic and Debate, is about reasoning and defending a position using logic.

Pros:

1. Uses real books (not just textbooks and workbooks)

2. Unit study approach to content

3. Ideal for families with children close in ability level

4. Content is arranged systematically

Cons:

1. Hard to use when students' ability levels vary

2. May feel less structured than traditional curriculum

Natural or Child-Directed Learning ('Unschooling')

The Natural Learning approach is all about learning without coercion. It is child or student-focused. Based on the premise that children learn best by doing, students are allowed to learn according to their interests, as parents facilitate activities and experiences. For example, a child learns basic arithmetic by helping to work out the monthly budget. A 13-year old child learns about electricity by wiring the house or repairing the television. In contrast to other homeschooling approaches, natural learning does not rely heavily on traditional textbooks or educational materials. Basically, the parents are responsible for being role models instead of authoritative teachers and for encouraging learning through positive affirmation. The child is responsible for asking questions and pursuing knowledge. The term "unschooling" means that the child is **not** being schooled in the usual regimented method.

Pros:

1. Freedom to pursue knowledge and skills according to interests

2. Flexibility

3. Hands-on learning

4. Focus on learning experiences

5. Saves time and money

6. Fosters love of learning

Cons:

1. May lack structure

2. Can lead to "spoiled" children who have a hard time being told "No"

3. Prone to learning and skill gaps

Homeschooling curricula based on the above approaches can be further classified into independent, instructor-dependent and mixed (interactive).

Independent. An independent curriculum contains all the material needed for the lesson and evaluation, including answer keys. Some examples are Wordly Wise, Alpha Omega and ACE.

Pros:

1. Minimal preparation for the teacher

2. Students can work at their own pace

3. Ideal for college or standardized exam preparation

Cons:

1. Minimal parent/educator involvement

2. Students may have difficulty remembering the material

Instructor-dependent. The instructor is essentially in-charge of the learning process and consults a manual for daily lessons. Examples are Sonlight and KONOS.

Pros:

1.   Can be used for multiple grade levels

2.   Works best for new homeschoolers and instructors

Cons:

1.   Preparing lessons can be time intensive.

Mixed (interactive). Mixed curricula fall between independent and instructor-dependent. The curriculum contains all the information for the lesson, which the instructor often reads along with the student. Instructors are also learning about the subject while they teach, increasing confidence when answering student questions. Some examples are Worldly Wise and Saxon Math.

Pros:

1. Minimal preparation needed for lesson plans

2. Active student and instructor involvement

Cons:

1. Spending an entire lesson with each student can take a lot of time if you have children of different ages and grade levels.

Legal Requirements For Homeschooling

Homeschooling has reemerged as a legally acceptable method of alternative education in several countries and in the fifty United States. Legal regulation of homeschooling varies significantly by location; some areas are more restrictive and consider home learning as an extension of the compulsory school system. Before homeschooling your child, it is important to understand laws, regulations and requirements (including record-keeping) in your area. In the U.S., consult your state education board or visit their website. Some states treat homeschooling like a regular private school education, while others have laws created particularly for homeschooling families.

Legal Requirements in the United Kingdom

Parents homeschooling their children are required to:

1. Recognize any special educational needs of your child

2. Notify the local authority (in writing) when removing your child from a special school

3. Ensure your child receives full-time education that matches their age and aptitude

4. Observe school hours, days or terms

Parents are NOT required to:

1. Be a qualified teacher

2.   Secure special permission from a school or local authority

3.   Give formal lessons

4.   Have a fixed timetable

Occasionally, the local authority may conduct "informal enquiries" to ensure that you are providing suitable homeschooling to your children. Representatives of local authorities have no right of access to your home, but you can invite them for a visit or meet outside the home. The child's presence is not required. As evidence, you can provide them with a written report and samples of your child's work.

Legal Requirements in the United States

Legal homeschooling requirements vary widely by state, and there is usually more than one option for homeschooling (with different requirements). The general trend in homeschooling is to ease the burden of requirements, and some states don't require notice. At the other end of the spectrum, some states require a credentialed instructor to teach the child or the child to be enrolled in a public school. No scientific studies currently support that heavier requirements lead to better results.

For simplicity's sake, here are three (3) broad categories of homeschooling regulations in the United States:

1) Homeschooling is considered a type of private school in some states (e.g. Texas and California). In this case, homeschooling families are required to follow laws that apply to private (or other) schools.

2) Homeschool requirements in some states (e.g. New Jersey) are set by the state's compulsory attendance statute without reference to "homeschooling."

3) Homeschool requirements in other states are set by statutes that specifically

refer to "homeschooling," "alternative instruction" or "private instruction."

States under the first category are usually the least restrictive in terms of homeschool requirements. Not sure which state homeschooling law you should follow? You should follow the law in the area in which you are currently present. Even if you are only in that particular state temporarily, and your legal residence is elsewhere, you are physically present in that state and are subject to its laws. This also applies to military families who are often on the move.

Understanding local homeschooling laws is not just to keep you out of jail. You want to know what federal or government aid (if any) you are entitled to and the extent of a homeschooled student's participation in public school activities, like team sports. For example, if your child has special education needs and you live in certain states that consider homeschooled children as private school students, you are eligible for the Individuals with Disabilities Education Act (IDEA) funding.

Securing Homeschool Requirements Example: Step by Step

This section will not cover the requirements for all fifty United States. Instead, we'll use Texas as an example. In Texas, home schools are considered private schools and are **not** regulated by the state. This means that you DO NOT need to register your child with the local school district. You do however need to comply with the following homeschool laws:

1.   Instruction must be bona fide (i.e., Instruction must be real, and you should not use homeschooling as an excuse to do something else)

2.   The curriculum must be in visual form (books, videos, other educational materials).

3. The curriculum must include the following subjects: reading, grammar, spelling, mathematics and good citizenship.

If your child is currently in public school, there are additional requirements:

1) Get a curriculum and withdraw your child from public school. See the previous section on selecting a curriculum.

2) Once you have a curriculum, write a letter of withdrawal to the school principal. Don't skip this step. Failure to send a written withdrawal may result in truancy charges. For proof of delivery, send your letter as certified mail with return receipt requested.

3) If the school asks for additional forms or a personal visit, simply send a letter of assurance. A letter of assurance is enough to satisfy compulsory attendance laws of cooperation with the school district.

4) You are not required to present an annual letter of assurance or to register with the local school district.

5) If the school district asks you to fill out a form (in addition to sending a letter of assurance), you can do so, but it is not recommended. The letter of assurance should be enough.

6) Begin homeschooling. Notes: You don't need teacher certification to homeschool your children, and you can use a tutor for instruction or send your child to the home of another homeschooling parent. Your children are also exempt from compulsory attendance laws.

The above example applies to the state of Texas only. In other states where homeschools are considered a type of private school, you will probably experience similar requirements. In states with more restrictive homeschool laws, expect additional requirements. Once you have the paperwork out of the way, I recommend that you join a local homeschool support group. Support groups are composed of homeschooling families like you, and they are great for building friendships, sharing ideas, encouragement, activities, family events, play dates and more. It's also a great way to keep up-to-date about home school laws and regulations in your area.

Now that you're homeschooling, it's important to enjoy your students and the learning experience. Flexibility is key to riding through the ups and downs. If something is not working, try something else, like the curriculum or method of instruction. Be realistic, and don't compare your students and teaching methods to the public school system. Focus on educational goals that meet your child's needs. And don't forget to ask for help from your support group during rough times.

Chapter 13: Selecting A Homeschooling Curriculum

Many parents love to create lesson plans and select the curriculum they will use to homeschool their children. These parents are confident, creative, and imaginative in their ability to teach their children at their home. This attitude makes it so much easier because the parents will be ready for school when they arrive.

It can be difficult for parents who are just starting to homeschool their children. There is no reason to be concerned if you are in this category. Many organizations offer approved and reliable services.

The Beginners Guide to Professional Homeschooling

accredited homeschool curriculums for sale. These include a pre-written teaching curriculum that includes both student workbooks and teaching manuals. These pre-made curriculums can be a great way to provide an education for your children, but it might not be as interesting or entertaining as an original one.

Pre-made curriculums can also be expensive. These curriculums come with all the necessary textbooks and reading materials required for each grade. Even the required books for your grade are included. You will only need pencils, paper, pens, and other supplies.

These curriculums can be used for a lot of work online. Online schools are available, so your child can go to school from home. These schools work in a similar way to regular public schools, as there are teachers and classes online. These classes will be just like public school for your child. These classes are interactive, so your child can ask questions and take part in answering them. This is an innovative way to allow your children homeschool. As you can see, this program is quite costly.

Computer homeschool programs are also available in certain areas. These programs can be conducted directly from public schools. These programs can be very affordable and free for some areas. You may be eligible for one or more of these programs. Your children could also receive a computer to use in homeschool classes.

If you decide to homeschool your children, you have many options. You will need to take into account many factors when choosing the best curriculum for you. In selecting the right curriculum or program for you, eligibility and availability are important factors. The most important aspect is the cost. You'll likely have to cut back if you don't have the funds.

The Beginners Guide to Professional Homeschooling

To pay for this, you can either save for a year or get a personal loan. It will be well worth it in the end.

Homeschooling Day

It can be difficult for homeschooling parents to know what kind of schedule their children should follow regarding schooling days. It can seem confusing at first, but it doesn't have to be a problem. When planning your teaching schedule, there are many things you should consider.

You and your children do not have to wake up at 3 AM if you homeschool. Many older children shouldn't be required to start school at a very early hour. They don't begin to notice the world until 10AM. Many children find 9AM to be a good time to get up and begin their day. Others children feel more at ease if they get up before 7 AM. Now you can follow your children's internal clock. You can start the day when your children are more alert, awake, and less grumpy.

You should ensure that they eat a good breakfast. People are more productive when their blood sugar levels are high. This doesn't mean they should eat a lot of sugar. Juice and milk can be accompanied by fruit, cheese, or an English muffin. They should have a balanced meal.

They should be awake by the time they finish breakfast so they can get started on their lessons. It's a good idea to start them with something they enjoy doing. Let them stretch after they have completed this subject. This is a great opportunity to use the bathroom and get something to eat.

The Beginners Guide to Professional Homeschooling

Drink.

Next, you will tackle one of your least favorite subjects. These must be tackled, regardless of whether you all hate it. It's not easy to find someone who finds geography interesting, but it is a common course in school curriculums. You and your children should try to make it enjoyable. Mid-morning is a good time to tackle geography if it is something your children hate. You'll find them awake and feeling energized after having had fun with one of your favorite subjects. Profit from it.

It may take up to an hour to complete the first two classes. The second class will likely be over by lunchtime depending on how long. You can give them a few extra minutes to read, listen to music, or do other things that they enjoy. It's time to move on to another favorite subject after lunch. These subjects should be placed later in the afternoon to keep your children awake and engaged. The afternoon hours can cause tiredness and sleepiness, which their boring subjects will be able to play on and put to bed. You can bet that they won't retain much of a subject if they are completely disinterested.

To avoid homework assignments, try to complete most of your work during school hours. You have the option to choose which days and hours you would like to homeschool according to your schedule.

This is one of the best things about homeschooling.

Homeschooling on a budget

You'll be surprised at how much it costs to ensure your kids are fully dressed for school if you have seen the supply lists. These supply lists can run upwards to $100. Add $300-500 per child if your children attend a school that needs uniforms.

The Beginners Guide to Professional Homeschooling

Parents choose to homeschool their children because they have financial problems. They don't need one financial problem to solve the other. These parents will want to find the best homeschool resources to reduce their financial burden.

Homeschooling can be a great way to save money on school supplies and teaching materials. You don't need to buy expensive textbooks for teaching at home.

You also have the option to decide on what supplies your children will need for their homeschooling work.

Here is a list with some of the most useful resources for homeschooling materials that are free or very low-cost.

* The Public Library: This library is the best you can find when homeschooling your kids. The library has something for everyone, regardless of age. There are books that teach, books for enjoyment, and music CDs and DVDs. Simply choose the best method for teaching you and sign it out with your library card.

You can check out all of these materials for free and use them in your homeschooling curriculum. You can plan your time so you are done with all materials borrowed from the library before they expire. If you have any questions, you can borrow them again. If you are looking for free homeschool materials, this is the place to look.

* Internet Websites: If you are looking for free homeschooling material, the Internet is your best resource. Many websites specialize in providing support for parents who homeschool their children.

The Beginners Guide to Professional Homeschooling

There are many sites that offer free materials. You can also look for libraries and paid memberships. However, it does not mean you will be able to get the best. You can do it! You can also print directly from your computer. You may not require any additional materials for lower grades.

These sites have tons of great material you can print right from your computer and make worksheets for your kids. You can also find learning aids and projects for every age group, which you can print and use as teaching material. This is all you need to print.

* On-hand Materials: These are magazines, newspapers, and other materials that you have in your possession for other purposes. These places contain many articles, photos, and other items. You can simply put them to work by including them in your teaching curriculum.

* Thrift Stores - If you are lucky enough to live near a thrift shop, you will find many items that you can use for homeschooling. You can find a little of everything in these shops. While not all items will be in great condition, even incomplete sets or things in poor condition, they can still be used for different purposes in your homeschool teaching. Keep in mind that thrift shops have very low prices.

* Garage and Yard Sales: These are also events that have items you can use in your homeschooling venture. You can find items at yard sales and garage sales that are affordable than thrift shops, and the prices are often negotiable. This is what it means.

The Beginners Guide to Professional Homeschooling

Because these people want to sell the items, not be stubborn and have to repackage them in the attic or basement. If you are unable to afford the full price of a product you like, you may be able to offer a lower price. Most times, you will be accepted.

Dollar Stores: These stores are still in business today after being around for more than 25 years. These stores are very popular because you can find almost anything and only one dollar per item. You can also get two items for one with a number of items. You'll be able to take home bags filled with items if you spend between ten and twenty dollars at a dollar store. It's almost as if you feel like you bought something and received your money.

You can find a variety of books, arts, crafts, and writing materials at dollar stores that you can use to homeschool your children. You'll be amazed at the variety of homeschooling materials and supplies you can find in these stores for as low as a dollar.

* Online auction sites: Many homeschooling materials are sold on websites like eBay. If you shop at the right time of year, you may be able to purchase complete sets of homeschooling materials. Many parents can't use the full programs purchased from a homeschool after they finish their year. Instead of throwing them away, they will put them up for purchase at a low price, or you can offer to bid.

These are great ways to get started in homeschooling with minimal out-of-pocket expenses. It's possible to find more ways to enhance your teaching skills as you go. You'll find that you can use everyday objects to teach your children. Homeschooling can be fun because you look around and find things that you can teach your kids about life and school subjects.

The Beginners Guide to Professional Homeschooling

You'll discover more items the more you look around. Most of the time, what you find yourself will be more enjoyable for your children and you. It's easier to do this with children younger than 10, as you can teach them anything that you have. You'll need to be more creative as they age, but it is still possible.

Chapter 14: Reduce Commitments Away From Home

Homeschooling, Yet Never Home

Homeschooling can make it difficult to be a responsible parent. This means that homeschoolers are more likely to go on a lot of outings each week, including swimming, skating and table tennis. These outings are often for the children's benefit, and are not to be confused with other obligations like homeschool group, prayer, Bible meetings, shopping, or church. It is clear that these trips often make us feel exhausted and can create an atmosphere of hectic' rather than 'heaven' in our homes. All this running around is normal, right? Is it normal? There is a difference.

Let's first acknowledge that not only is the homeschooler always on the move, taking their children to different activities throughout the week. This is the norm in western society. It's not only children's activities that are being rushed, but also adults who want to enjoy their entire quota of entertainment and recreation. Let's take a moment to reflect on how this all happened over the past five or six decades. Did our parents drive our parents to different activities almost every day when they were younger? It is unlikely. It was unlikely that the family owned a car, and they probably wouldn't have owned two. It was rare for children to drive to school or to any other activity. Weekend activities or after-school activities were often limited to scouts or guides or a season's sport. Sunday school and church attendance were the highlights of the week. Sunday school was rare. How have things changed since then? Have these changes possibly led to an increase in stress for parents today?

The higher standard of living is one change. Before then, few mothers worked.

Two cars per family is now considered normal and necessary for modern working mothers. However, stay-at home mothers also want their own car. They can then take their children and themselves around without waiting for Father to return from work. The parents can live their lives independently of one another. . .

Another thing that has changed is the wide range of activities available and their affordability. They are also affordable for those who believe they are important. There are many venues nearby for horse-riding, jazz, bootcooting and pottery, as well as music, drama, dance, ballroom dancing, BMX racing, martial art, and any other sport. These activities were not available to our parents when we were children. There are now versions for children as young as three. Your little girl can look adorable in a dancing costume or on top of a pony. Kindagym offers a swimming class for babies. If he is able to walk, he may be able to go.

Clubs that used to be exclusively for boys now welcome girls. Girls' soccer, girls' cricket, girls' football are all available. The competition season is almost always open, thanks to night-time and Sunday sports, as well as indoor sport complexes. Play and pay are now possible all year.

The west is blessed with a wide range of activities outside the home. It is natural to eat a lot when there are so many options. The bumper stickers that suggest mother's new role as 'chauffeur" may have been familiar to you. One bumper sticker simply states "Mum's Taxi", while another says "If a Mother's Place is at Home, why am I always in the car?" This is a great question for a Christian homeschooling mom.

First, I have to make another confession. With a certain pride years ago, I used to tell people that even though we were homeschoolers, we almost never went home. Why was I saying such a thing? Why was this true? This is because I didn't want to give the impression that homeschooling means separating children from the "real world". The idea of homeschooling was misunderstood in the general population, who believed such children were lacking 'socialization'. So I quickly dispelled the idea that my children were socially isolated and made it clear that we were always out and about and interacting with the outside world. What a fool I was! How unscriptural.

The Bible Does Not Date

God may see our excess commitments outside of the home as important. These verses are on the topic:

Titus 2:4,5

"That they might teach young women to be sober and to love their husbands and their children.

To be discrete, chaste and keepers at their home.

1 Timothy 5:11-14

"But the younger widows reject: For when they have started to wax wanton about Christ, they will get married.

They are condemned to damnation for having abandoned their first faith.

They learn to be inactive, wandering from one house to the next; but not only are they idle, but also tattlers and busybodies who speak things they shouldn't.

Therefore, I will see that the younger women marry and have children.

What does the Lord say through the Apostle Paul in these passages of scripture? Titus makes it clear that a Christian mother must be a keeper of the home and that her role is equally important as loving her children and husband. It is not that the mother does not venture out of her course. However, she will tell you that she rarely lets herself go from home, and only for legitimate reasons such as shopping, church, or important educational reasons. She enjoys being at home and has taught her children not to want to leave.

The above passage is from Paul's first letter addressed to Timothy and focuses on the case of young widows. Its message is relevant today because young widows are independent, something Paul called a bad situation. Even though times have changed significantly since Paul's time, his warning is still relevant today. Modern Christian mothers may be tempted to wander from one house to another, while neglecting their homes and gossiping in the name 'fellowship. Paul says this is acting as if you are a widow without any home responsibilities. Is it possible to do this simply because we have money and a car? How many divorces are caused by the wives neglecting the home, if only the truth could be known? Neglecting the home means neglecting her husband and children. According to the Bible, such neglect can lead to God's word being blasphemed and our enemies to speak reproachfully. These are serious charges! These are serious charges! It's almost impossible to maintain a house well if you are not there. This is known as stress.

Subtle Neglect

The modern society is focused on the fact that people are mobile and home-based. It is easy to hide a lot of neglect and not notice how we are depriving our children and ourselves of our mother roles. This is something I've done, and here's a proof:

It's Monday. It is Monday. You rush through breakfast, devotions, and dishes. Then, you set the washer on and race out with your children to iceskating. You reach the rink at 10:00 am by picking up two of your friends' children. Although you've packed sandwiches and a cup of coffee, the children arrive at the rink thirsty. The cafeteria fries smell delicious, so it ends up costing you a lot. You've had a lot of fun with your friends and the children, and they have had a blast. You're now heading home and need to stop by the supermarket to pick up a few items. You buy a few more necessities. You arrive at your friend's house in the middle of the afternoon to drop off her children. She invites you to join her for a cup of tea and a chat. You tell yourself you would love to but it's impossible to stop. You realize that you will not have enough time to cook dinner when your husband comes home. So that everyone has something hot for dinner at the dinner hour, you drive to the pizza pick up and get home right before your husband arrives. You make a sandwich for your baby and then put him to sleep. Then you dry the laundry in the dryer because you aren't home. The end of another exhausting day is over when your husband pulls into the driveway. Have you got an evening meeting?

I remember many days as a homeschooling mom. Do you? At the time, I didn't think I was robbing my family. To give my children an extensive education, I believed I was making a huge personal sacrifice. My husband was being robbed by me. I was neglecting my spiritual well-being and that of the children. My husband was paying me a lot more for my home (petrol, car, skate costs, food and drink, running clothes dryers, pizza), but I was also taking his orderly home, my attention, my peace, and my serenity away by not maintaining it. Instead of being a quiet and meek wife, he would return home to a frazzled wife. He was being robbed.

It is possible to neglect your home and still be at home. Television used to be the largest time thief in many households. But that is no longer the case. Recently, I read of Christian mothers confessing that they spend hours a day on the internet and are almost unable to stop. This is a problem for some.

These things are not meant to be a criticism of the technology we have today. (As a mother of a large family, I am grateful for my clothes dryer!) Technology is not to blame, but it is important that we recognize the dangers of misuse of technology.

High-Mobility Society

Today's technology has enabled us to move at a level never seen before in human history. An engineer friend from Europe told me about a conference he attended at Paris' international airport. He arrived in Paris from many countries and flew in half an hour before the conference started. Large Boeing jets were visible from the meeting room's windows, taking off and landing every few minutes. He was able to take a flight to his capital city, arriving in time to eat lunch. This is certainly speed and mobility! Could it be stress?

You might be like me and know people who regularly go to the shops. Sometimes, they claim they go to the shops because they're bored at home. One of them tells me she shops because it is her hobby. Society has altered its expectations of social interaction and mobility. It's easy to fall into the trap of conforming to what is now considered normal. Today, normal is being redefined almost every day. The world is mixing normal today. What was 'normal' once?

Do you remember the books "Little House on the Prairie?" Laura Ingalls Wilder wrote about her childhood in the American countryside during the second half of the nineteenth century. Because they were rare, visits and social events were treasured memories. Even though life was busy, it was slow and easy. The home was the center of life. Family members were closely connected by their love and shared the responsibility for the upkeep of the home. Going out could be a simple matter of going somewhere near enough to walk or a family affair that involved Pa pulling the wagon and horse. Even though mothers might have been tempted to spend time at the home of a neighbor, there weren't any fast-food outlets that would allow them to cook the evening meal. In days past, there was less social interaction outside of the home, and there were fewer modern social evils like drugs and pornography. It makes me wonder if there is a connection.

Are Our Children Require Multiple Activities?

We have examined how an out-of-home homeschooling mom can lose focus on her Biblical role and stress. Others may argue that education should be a broad range of experiences for our children. You might argue that this will encourage their interest and help them discover the things they enjoy and are good at.

Your children will not complain about the activities that you offer them. If we homeschool because God has called us to, then we need to consider God's agenda before we allow our children to enjoy it.

There may not be anything wrong with the sports or activities your children have participated in. According to the Bible, "all things can be lawful for me but not all things edify." 1 Corinthians 10:23 It is possible, however, that too many activities could undermine the spiritual values that we try so hard to teach.

Let me share some examples. The child may develop a need to be carried around for enrichment. You could quickly get the impression that your baby's nap or housework is more important than his tennis game.

Second, your child's environment and interactions with others can have an impact on their behavior. Are there any unwholesome background music that you don't like? Are all of the people present Christians? It is possible that you won't be able or able to see your child enough during the activity to notice any unwanted effects.

Third, you may be putting him on a course that could distract from his desire to serve the Lord. As in many western countries, Australia is a nation that worships sport. Is this how you are defining yourself in this area? Do you unwittingly tell your child, through your actions, that recreation is more important than concern about the lost? That he should purchase a new hockey stick or Bibles for poor believers in other nations? Is recreation and spirituality in the right balance? "Bodily exercise is not profitable; but godliness is beneficial to all things. It promises the life that is now and that which will come. "(1 Timothy 4:8)

It is obvious that commercial sports are no longer played for fun. They are played with an aggressive, win-at-all costs attitude. While this does not mean that children shouldn't be involved in sports, it does mean that we need to be more careful about where our focus is. We don't want to stress to our children that life is about satisfying the flesh or pleasure-seeking, rather than seeking eternal value. To avoid frustrating our children, we must look ahead and see where a sport or activity will lead. Are competitors expected to wear clothes that you might consider immodest? Although lawn bowls is considered a gentle and dignified game, it is also played in an environment that allows for the consumption of alcoholic beverages. Billiards and darts are also subject to this rule. The Bible says that the games are legal for us to play. But for our children's benefit, let's use wisdom.

The greatest temptation comes to the child who excels in a sport. We must communicate the right balance with our children or we could endanger their souls.

A common but often overlooked effect of overscheduling our children's lives with activities is their excessive tiredness. Here is an excerpt from Inda Schaenen's secular book, "The 7 O'clock Bedtime".

"A child who hurries from one place to another, without any regard for a set routine or a reasonable bedtime, is not living her life. Even if she begs for entertainment and activities, she is being pulled along by a freight train. It is likely that the freight she is carrying isn't hers; it belongs to those in her life who have their agenda. . . Poor sleep is caused by constant hurrying, this racing headlong through life, from activity to activity, and ending with a period where you are numbing your attention to the television or the so-called educational game on the computer. Poor sleep leads to daytime problems and this cycle continues.

Homeschoolers might feel that the "agenda" of adults is to make their child shine above all others. This could 'justify' homeschooling. This will allow you to examine your motives for enrolling your children into too many activities and, if it is, confess your pride to Jesus Christ.

You can consult your husband if you feel that you need to reduce outside commitments. You can both ask God to help you organize this area of life. It might be possible to decide on a single type of recreation that everyone can enjoy together. You might consider asking your husband to bring a music teacher to your home to teach lessons. This will minimize disruption to your daily routine. If we are persistent in looking for solutions, there will be them.

It is a fact that outside commitments rob us of more time than the engagement itself. Our children spend a lot of time in the car, which is largely wasted time. It's too fast for children to see the outside and learn anything from it. Traveling is exhausting for everyone. Listening to the Bible on audio or singing together hymns could be a good way to use travel time, especially for necessary journeys.

Two-fold reasons outside commitments can drain us are: they take up time and energy and leave us with a lot to do at home. Homeschooling parents must be mindful of their priorities and value their God-given roles. We should also limit our commitments to outside parties. This will help us to get rid of bad habits that can undermine our spiritual goals and relieve us of much stress.

Chapter 15: Should You Homeschool?

This is a question that many people ask themselves, and it's a hard question. Many people worry about their child's reaction to homeschooling, but that's not usually the most important thing. Taking out your child after they've been in public or private school for a very long time can be very hard on both of you. So it's important to ask yourself if it's worth it. If they're already built friendships and social connections it may not be the best idea. However, there are reasons that are good enough.

The 10 Questions:

Homeschooling is done within reason, and it has to be doable. So ask yourself all the questions that you need to before you make a decision on the matter. Here is a list of questions you should ask yourself if you're thinking about homeschooling your child:

Are they happy where they are?

This is an important question to ask yourself. Taking your child out even though they're happy where they are can cause problems. There are reasons that you can take them out despite being happy, but their happiness will actually affect both their home life as well as their academic success. So don't take your child out to homeschool them without a reason that is suitable.

Are you happy with the education they're receiving?

If you aren't happy with the education hat your child is receiving, then something needs to be done. You either need to find them a new school, or you need to homeschool them. Education is important because it helps to decide your child's future. If you see that your child is falling behind then make an effort to help them. That effort could be homeschooling.

Can you handle homeschooling your child?

One important aspect about homeschooling is being able to handle it. Homeschooling isn't possible if you're also keeping a job. You need to have the time to put into homeschooling your child. So make sure that you have the time and the patience to homeschool. If you're having issues getting along with your child, homeschooling may not be the best option. However, if you do get along with your child homeschooling is a viable option.

Are they getting hurt where they are? Mentally, physically, or educationally?

Bullying is a huge issue in schools today, and that's for public and private schools. So ask yourself if your child is being hurt in anyway. If they aren't getting the education they need, are coming home crying because of emotional distress, or being physically harmed, homeschooling may be a better option. Sometimes this pain can also come from teachers. If they're being hurt, take them out of the environment.

Are they succeeding academically in a traditional option?

The point of sending your child to school is so they can learn. Their grades will tell you if they're learning properly or not, so make sure to pay attention. If they're in public or private school and just can't keep up the grades, then a traditional school option just isn't for them. Either get a tutor or try homeschooling your child.

Is there a religious reason you wish to take them out?

Religion is sometimes a major reason why parents decide to homeschool their child. In public schools religion is not allowed, but there are private school options if you want them to have a religious upbringing. This is a viable option for anyone who doesn't have the time to homeschool but still wants religion to be an influence on their educational experience. Religion can't be the only reason you homeschool your child, but it is a large deciding factor.

How old are they?

When a child is younger it can be easier to take them out of a traditional schooling option and put them into homeschooling. They haven't made the deep connections to their friends or environment that older children have. That isn't to say just because they're older that they can't be homeschooled, but it may take more serious reasons to want to take them out. You don't want your child to become depressed because it will affect both their academic and mental state.

Is there a family reason you wish to take them out?

It's been proven that traditional school options for the most part devalue the family unit. They don't put as much importance on blood and family as many families approve of. Traditional educational options usually say that the community is the most important structure in their life, but many parents don't approve of it. You can take your child out for family reasons, and that way strengthen your family as a whole.

Do you have the time?

There is no getting around it: If you don't have the time to homeschool your child, you can't do it. So make sure that you have the time to spend on their education, or they're better off being left where they are or being put into a different school if you must. Working a job and homeschooling your child doesn't work. It'll just make you more tired, and it won't give them the time they need to learn the material and prosper.

Can you provide them with social interaction outside of the home?

Social interaction is important in any child's life. You have to be able to provide social interaction outside of the home, preferably with people of their age group, if you want to homeschool your child. If they become bored easily or feel cut off from everyone because you're homeschooling them, they won't do well.

Will They Prosper?

An important question to any parent considering homeschooling is if your child will prosper doing it. If they won't prosper, it's usually better to leave them where they are. You don't want to take their future and education in your hands if you don't think they can succeed. Here are five simple questions you can ask yourself to figure out if your child will prosper:

The 5 Questions:

Do they take education seriously?

A child that is homeschooled has to take education seriously or they'll try to slack off every chance they get. If they don't want to learn, you're going to have a hard time teaching them. You want them to be able to sit there and do their work. If you don't think they'll take your instruction seriously or their education, then you may want to leave it to the professionals. Left in a traditional option they'll have no choice but to listen at least a little.

Do they like spending time with their family?

When a child is homeschooled it means that they're spending a lot of time at their house and with their family. A child that is homeschooled shouldn't have a hard time trying to get along with siblings, parents, or anyone else that lives in the household. If they do have problems, you may find that they spend more time arguing and fighting than actually getting any work done.

Do they crave interaction?

Every child craves interaction to a point, but some do so more than others. If your child participates in a school related sport, club, or other activity, you may not want to take them away from it. The last thing you need is your child to become depressed being homeschooled because it won't work out well for them or you.

Do they respect you?

If you're going to homeschool your child, you need to make sure they hold some sort of respect for you. They may respect others before they respect you. You can't teach a child that is constantly undermining your authority. If they can't take you seriously, they won't take the education you're trying to give them seriously.

Do you think they can work on their own?

Teachers are able to let students have time to work on their own, either in groups or individually. You have to ask yourself if you think that you can trust your child to work on their own. Having to watch them every morning until they're done in the afternoon at every minute, it's not going to work out. You'll only end up despising your choice, and it can cause a rift between you and your child.

Chapter 16: The Legalities

This is one of the most important and worried about aspects of homeschooling. Depending on which state you are in, there will be different rules. Following the rules is important.

There is a specific website dedicated to legalities in America from state-to-state and international homeschooling, among many other things. This site is found at https://www.HSLDA.org.

Because laws are prone to change, I am not going to spell out each states legal requirements. Instead we are going to cover accessing the information necessary to live by the laws of your state, and then we will discuss what some of the requirements entail and how you can do your part to make sure you are abiding by the homeschooling legal requirements of your state.

The first thing you will want to do, before anything else, is join HSLDA. Beyond giving amazing resources to help you live by the law, they will also help you and represent you legally when you face problems in your state.

On HSLDA's website they have a map of the U.S. (you can also access legal help for other countries) where you can pick your state and it will give you details on how to legally homeschool in your state. Some states are very "green" meaning there is a lot of homeschooling freedom and very little requirements. Some are more "red" and require a lot more of homeschooling families.

I encourage you to read the full page for your state so that you can understand what your options are before making a decision. We will discuss your different options and the pros and cons.

Homeschool Statute

This option simply allows you to educate your child in your home. You must be a parent or legal guardian. Depending on the state you may or may not have requirements to notify the state, seek approval, test, file forms, or have teacher qualifications.

In some states you will be required to file a one-time affidavit of intent to homeschool. You may also be required to file a new one every year. Your children may also be required to take an annual assessment every year or submit a portfolio of the work they have accomplished.

Some states require specific subjects. This can be simple requirements. For example: reading, writing, spelling, grammar, geography, arithmetic, and U.S. History. This could also be way more in depth. In New York, for example, requirements range from patriotism to traffic safety, arithmetic to U.S. history, music to physical education, and library skills to electives (3 credits).

Private Tutor or Certified Teacher

Some states have the option of homeschooling using a private tutor or a certified teacher. Most states require that a private tutor have state-based teacher certification. If you, as the parent, are a certified teacher then you can homeschool in a lot of states with no oversight. You can also hire an instructor for your children that has a teaching certificate. Some states, such as California, will require you to provide instruction for your children for a certain amount time between the hours of 8am and 4pm. They may also require your child to "attend" 175 days of school.

Umbrella Schools

Umbrella school are referred to in many different ways. They are also known as church schools or satellite schools. These types of schools work by essentially providing an umbrella of requirements that offer you the freedom to do what you would like outside of a state's requirements. For example, your umbrella school may require you to keep attendance records and a portfolio, but because you are enrolled in an umbrella school you are not required to take yearly assessments in your state. Each umbrella school is different, so it is important to do your research when searching for one. They can also provide student ID cards, field trip opportunities, and more.

Private School

Considering we discussed what a private school is in chapter 3, you may be confused at learning this is also a way to homeschool. You can make this work by starting your own home-based private school and enrolling your children in your "private school." You can also find existing home-based private school programs that will function much like an umbrella school.

Independent School

This is similar to a satellite school in that you join with one or more other homeschooling families to create minimal requirements for your "independent school" and aim to comply with statutory requirements. In states like Delaware they will refer to it as a "multi-family homeschool." In this case, the multi-family homeschool will appoint one member to coordinate and act as liaison to the Department of Education. They are responsible for submitting attendance and enrollment information.

The Importance of Recordkeeping

You will see this section added to every "state" page on the HSLDA website. This is important because, although you may not be required to keep records or a portfolio, you may need it in an emergency. Believe it or not, homeschoolers have CPS called on them. Not because they are doing anything wrong, but because those around them do not understand the legal homeschooling rights that they are abiding by. When this happens, it is always a good idea to have records on hand to show that your children are not simply truant.

You will also be grateful you organized a portfolio when your child is putting together paperwork for acceptance into college. Sometimes universities will ask for a sample of your child's work to get an idea of their work ethic, abilities, and experiences. In these situations, you will be glad you kept records!

Chapter 17: Snow Days Keeping Your Kids On Task Even During Snow Days

For home school families, snow days can be a challenge. Whether you choose to follow your local public school's schedule when it comes to snow days or you choose to home educate even during snow storms and blizzards, you'll need to come up with a way of keeping your children entertained and busy. Snowy weather is fun to play in, but there will be days when you have to keep your kids inside. This presents a challenge, especially if you live in an area with long winters. Even the best of students can grow weary and tired of working on the same projects in the same room.

There are a number of ways you can entertain your kids and keep them busy during the winter months:

*Go on scavenger hunts in your house. Give each child a list of questions they must find the answers to. Let them have access to computers or have them only look through books. Then reward each child with a special treat, prize, or movie after they've found all of the answers. You could even do themed scavenger hunts such as "questions about history" or "famous authors." For younger kids, do actual item scavenger hunts and require them to find things like a feather, a penny, or even a photograph.

*Make every day an art project day. Do you have an oversized craft box you need to start downsizing? Why not let your kids explore it and get creative? Spend an entire day making project after project until you've had your fill of arts and crafts.

*Play board games. Sound pretty simple? That might be true, but it's easy for board games to get buried under layers of dust with the promise of "We'll play them later." Make "later" be "today." Pull out your kids' favorite board games and spend an entire afternoon playing them. If you get bored with the regular rules, get creative! Make up your own rules or even combine the rules of several games to make up more interesting gameplay.

*Go roller skating in your garage or in yourbasement.Don't forget your knee pads and helmets.

*Look through old family albums.

*Make a scrapbook.

*Tackle an uninteresting chore. Put on some music to make it fun. Dance around and laugh while you clean or sort through things.

*Let each child decorate a square of fabric. Let them embroider or paint the squares. Then, use your sewing machine to combine the squares into a small quilt.

*Write a story together. Have each child write a paragraph of a story before passing it on to the next person. This is an interesting way to make up an adventure without knowing where the story is going to end up. For example, one person may start a paragraph about a medieval princess but by the time the story finishes, it could be about a magical carrot named Sam.

*Share old memories. Talk about favorite family vacations, silly moments, or other interesting things you remember.

*Plan a fantasy vacation. Is there a place you've always wanted to visit but haven't had the chance? Put together a folder of possible trips for the future. Figure out the cost of tickets or renting a car, the day's excursions, and even the cost of food. Then start a small savings jar where you can start saving up for your vacation.

*Make a trip to the library. Check out books, movies, and even CDs to listen to while you're stuck inside on your snow day.

*Have a pajama day. Let each child stay in their pajamas all day long. Pile blankets and pillows in the living room. Don't forget the stuffed animals! Read story books, tell stories, and even watch movies.

*Put on a play. Let your kids act out their favorite story or movie. Put on any costumes you have sitting around. This is a great time to break out your Halloween costumes! Who said you could only wear your costumes one day a year? Many moms also stock up on costumes the week after Halloween when they may be discounted 25%, 50%, or even 75%! Costumes are a fun and entertaining way to spend a day and give your kids something fun to experience that they don't get to enjoy every day.

Remember that no matter what you decide to do, pick activities that interest and excite your child. It's easy to come up with fun things to do once you let your imagination run wild. Remember that it's **okay** to take a day off and do fun things that don't necessarily involve structured plans or worksheet pages. It's okay. Sometimes just spending time together as a family and having fun bonding is just as important as the things your child learns from his schoolbooks.

Falling behind or falling ahead
How to handle being "behind" or "ahead" in your scheduled work

"We're ahead about two units, so we're taking the next month off from teaching."

"Jessie is really behind in math, so we've been doing lessons twice a day."

"Oh, well, my son is really advanced so he's ahead in reading."

Have you ever heard your peers say things like this? Have you maybe uttered similar statements yourself? Many home school parents, especially **new** home school parents, get hung up on being "behind" or "ahead" when it comes to schoolwork.

This is an especially big deal for families who might miss a lesson or two due to illness, a death in the family, or even a mid-year move.

In my experience, the idea of being "ahead" or "behind" is unnecessary. These are terms adopted from the public school system which is on a tight, limited schedule. There are only so many school days for public school to teach, so for them, the idea of being ahead or behind is very important. For home school families who have flexible, lenient schedules, these ideas aren't nearly as important.

Instead of focusing on whether your child is at the same level as his best friend, focus on making sure your child has regular, thorough instruction. You don't need to make your child do eight math lessons a day just to make sure he's "ahead." It's okay to just do one lesson a day or even one lesson every other day.

One of the biggest perks of home education is that you remove the competition from your child's life. There **isn't** that pressure to have a "gifted" child. All children are gifted especially in the eyes of their parents. Instead of worrying that your child isn't as far ahead academically as his peers or that he's not as smart as another home schooled child, focus on making sure your child is having fun learning and that you're teaching things that interest him.

If your child struggles with reading, for example, don't feel like you need to tell your peers, "My son is behind in reading." All children learn at different speeds and all children have different strengths. This is one of the most beautiful things about home education. You can focus on your child's strengths and help him become stronger in his weak areas. Instead of feeling like your child is behind in reading, instead encourage your child for trying so hard and continue to work with him.

Unfortunately, the idea of whether a child is "behind" or "ahead" is one of those things home school moms tend to worry about and yes, this is enough to make you go crazy. Even if you know in your heart that your child is perfect just the way he is, there may be a little piece of you that just wishes your child was **amazing** at something. As a fellow mother and as your friend, I'll be honest and say that you have to let those feelings go.

There's no room for disappointment in parenting. If you express disappointment in your child's weaknesses, he'll remember for the rest of his life. Instead of being sad that your five-year-old struggles with addition, why not work on introducing some new ways to learn math? Maybe he doesn't like workbooks. Instead of forcing him to sit through printed number worksheets, try counting Legos. You could download some math apps to your phone or iPad and go through those. You can even practice telling time on your clock.

Don't tell your child "I wish you were better at this" or "I don't know why you aren't getting this." Just focus on helping your child learn in different ways.

Again, one of the beautiful things about home schooling is that you don't have to be perfect and neither do your children. It's okay to have flaws and weaknesses. We all do. Instead of focusing on your child being behind, though, focus on helping him excel. Just rip the words "behind" and "ahead" from your vocabulary and instead focus on works like "exceed" and "improve." Those are things you want for your child, after all. You want him to exceed in everything he tries and to improve those areas where he tends to struggle. As a fantastic, kick-booty home school mom, you've got it covered. You can do it.

Chapter 18: What If My Kid Won't Learn From Me?

"My kids behave like angels for their teachers, but they'll never learn from me!" We hear this a lot from would-be homeschool parents. Here's the thing: kids generally don't have a choice in school. They have to fall in line and do the work. The consequences for not doing so are pretty big. No one wants to go to the principal's office or lose recess. At home, you are the principal, but they know you and your weaknesses, and they will exploit them! Kidding . . . kind of. But it's natural for kids to push boundaries with parents. It's healthy even. The trick is to balance this boundary pushing with the structure you feel necessary to accomplish your educational goals.

It's vital to remember that the primary determiner of home education success is the parent's attitude. This is what will help your kids go along with this homeschooling scheme. Your attitude will set the tone for every single experience, so it's important to do whatever it takes to begin teaching from a place of peace, calm, and confidence.

Ask yourself helpful questions: What does it take for me to feel comfortable and at ease while doing school at home? Do I need it clean? Do I need order and schedules and routines? Do I need more sleep? Do I need quiet? Do I need to get up earlier so I can have an hour of "me time" to mentally prepare before the krakens awake?

I suggest preparing a list of things that make you immediately stressed upon waking. Is there anything on that list that you can let go for the time being? Yes? Good, cross them off. With the remaining items, figure out how to tackle them before they're driving you crazy. If necessary, spend a few days working on this before diving into your new academic routine. Household care is a valuable skill, as is self-care. Modeling self-care is perhaps one of the most important life lessons you can teach, so please don't discount this as real learning.

Once you're comfortable in your home and feel good about your jumping off point, it's time to establish or reaffirm trust between you and your new students. Many will be very skeptical. The nature of the traditional school model usually keeps home and school very separate. Kids associate learning with teachers, desks, and chalk boards. They might be doubtful that you are qualified. You yourself might be doubtful. But please listen: YOU CAN DO THIS!

The important thing to understand is that education at home will likely look very different than the traditional school model. Let's break it down a little with some quick practical tips to get your kids on your side and ready to learn!

1. Approach this as an experiment in home learning, not as a dictatorship.

Many experienced home educators have found that viewing themselves as a facilitator of learning rather than a "teacher" works well. Sit down with your kids and tell them something like this: "I'm new here, too. We're in this together. We have our goals set and now we need to move toward them together. It's very true that I might not know as much as your teacher does about prepositions, but together we can look up answers and learn it. I really want you to feel good about this and be motivated to learn and I'm going to support you in that. Think of me like your coach. I'm going to give you tips but I can't be out on the field with you. I'm here to help you figure out how to be successful in this game, but I can't carry the ball to the goal line. That's your job. I'm just here to help you learn how to do it well in your own way."

In order for them to believe you, you might ask them to teach you something. Video games are a great way to start. Let them guide you, laugh at your mistakes, and thank them for being patient with you. Analyze how they teach you, what they get excited about, and then use this knowledge as you move forward.

Nothing will kill the family learning spirit more than you having to yell through your tears and theirs to finish a math worksheet. They might technically finish it, but did they learn? And was there damage done to your relationship? Was it worth it? Could you have backed off and tried another approach? Could it have waited until tomorrow? Was the child hungry? Tired? Antsy? Scared? Were you? All those little issues certainly can affect learning. Solve those problems first, then settle down for learning. And if all else fails, give them a hug and a smile, and try again tomorrow.

2. Lead by example.

Another amazing trick that I've learned along the way is to set the example for learning. When I was struggling to get one of my children motivated to pick up a new subject, I got tired of begging them to learn. So instead, based on advice from others, I decided to take up a new hobby. Sculpting. Faces. Yep, pretty random. I had only very basic knowledge from watching my grandmother. I purchased a book on Amazon and the necessary supplies, which were a few boxes of clay and a small set of metal tools. I was determined to learn to sculpt a face. I told kids that school was canceled for the day and they could do whatever they wanted as long as they were in the room with me and not on screens. I set up all my supplies on the kitchen counter and quietly began learning. It took only thirty minutes before all three kids were sitting with me. One quietly drove his monster trucks over Play-doh, but the other two asked for some of my clay. Hoping this would be the case, I'd also purchased a more kid-friendly sculpting book and conveniently had it on the counter as well.

They took the bait. We spent the entire day working on sculpting. I verbalized my frustrations but also talked through how I would overcome them and how learning a new thing is hard and takes time but it's a fun challenge. We all laughed at my Neanderthal-looking forehead and jaw lines. The kids absently ate their lunches while still working on sculptures. Bedtime got pushed back. We were in deep and it was amazing. As the days went on, the kids' interest in sculpting waned, but they would get notebooks or novels and sit by me as we drank tea and worked away. This is one of my very fondest homeschooling memories. And it cost all of $50. I did finally sculpt a face that vaguely resembled Homo Sapiens. While my kids probably won't be Michelangelos, they did come to understand that learning doesn't have to feel like torture, and that when you're really interested in something, time flies. They saw that new things are hard, and they witnessed my frustration, but they also saw that persistence and grit are key to success.

If you're daunted by the task of homeschooling right now, I'd advise you to do something similar to our sculpting experience. It might help you grasp the big picture.

If you find your child really pushing back on the assigned learning, please remember that learning comes in all shapes and sizes. Don't get caught up in the idea that learning has to look like memorizing vast volumes of facts. Learning can look like measuring flour to bake cookies, understanding why the cookies failed, trying again, and learning that failure is part of the process. Learning can look like sculpting a face or building a Lego set. If you find yourself in the midst of a power struggle, my advice is to take a step back and suggest alternative learning ideas. Find a way to make this fun for you as well. It's hugely important that you enjoy this experience. You don't have to enjoy it every minute, but in general, you need to feel positive about it.

3. Don't put mandatory time frames on learning.

Two hours a day is likely quite enough in the home setting for middle schoolers and lower to complete their schoolwork. Traditional schools, by necessity, spend a lot of time on things like lining up, walking, sitting down, handing things out, settling in, and transitioning. You won't have any of this.

When you're learning at home with one-on-one instruction, it goes faster and they absorb more. What might take them two or three lessons in traditional school might only take 30 or 45 minutes of one-on-one instruction. This is because you can see exactly where the errors are and instantly correct them. In the classroom setting, often these errors aren't apparent until after the assignment has been graded and handed back and then it's sometimes too late—the class has moved on. This is simply not an issue in the home setting. We recommend correcting any worksheets immediately and then re-doing the areas that had mistakes. Make sure they have a good grasp of the concept. If not, head to the internet for other tutorials.

Typical homeschoolers in our group spend about 1-3 hours, 4-5 days a week on formal, sit-down schoolwork. And yet they are right on par with peers in standardized testing. So it's definitely possible to get a full, robust education in this shorter time span.

4. Short intervals with lots of breaks.
It's not natural for kids to sit for hours at a time. We know they can do it in school, but it's going to be doubly hard at home. We recommend limiting seat time to 20-35 minutes for younger students. After

each assignment, let them have some free time while you take some free time, too. This can be as short as 10-20 minutes, but it's so much easier than trying to push through without stopping. When it's time to call them back to school, give a few warnings, like, "Hey, let's do reading when you're at a stopping point in your puzzle, probably in 5-10 minutes." Let them transition out of their current activity as naturally as possible. Giving them a little bit of freedom in their own time management can help lower resistance to formal learning time.

5. Give them autonomy and choice.

We recommend a checklist system to allow children the freedom to choose which task to do first. See the chapter on schedule ideas for a full checklist example. Let's be honest—no one likes being told what to do and when to do it. There aren't a lot of reasons that you would need to implement a strict schedule in the home unless you have online classes starting at a particular time. This is a small and easy way to give kids freedom and a little bit of power in their lives and it can pay dividends in lowering their resistance to learning.

6. Keep it cozy (hygge homeschooling).

We like to keep our home school feeling quite homey and cozy. In the beginning, I set up a cool schoolroom downstairs in our house. The entire living space was dedicated to school materials. Each kid had a nice desk in front of a window and a large shelf beside it so their spaces were divided up like cubicles, but with a great views! We had a dedicated art table, as well as a round table where they sat with me for one-on-one time. It was so lovely, with nice rugs, awesome shelves, cool posters, and good light. I spent a bit of time and money setting it all up. Guess where we did school today? On our kitchen counter, sticky with syrup and crunchy with toast crumbs. Sometimes we migrate to the couch also.

For some reason, forcing my kids to march downstairs at a specific time every morning felt a little off for us. It certainly felt like a large undertaking for me. When we were down there I was unable to do any other household chores. I had to dedicate that time entirely to schooling. The thing is, my kids don't need my complete attention all of the time, so a lot of it was just sitting down there waiting for a question. I felt frustrated and often ended up nagging them to hurry because I felt the clock ticking on my other tasks for the day.

After Christmas one year we somehow migrated upstairs. We eat breakfast and then they grab their computers and generally do their online math class. I clean up from breakfast and sometimes prep lunch, but I'm instantly available for questions. I enjoy feeling like schoolwork is just part of our daily life and not something we have to stop and do, it takes some pressure off. After math, sometimes they continue on with their typing lessons at the counter or they'll move to the couch for reading and writing. They use notebooks or clipboards if needed, or sit on the floor and use the coffee tables. Each child now has a basket with all of their supplies that we tuck away when we're finished. Easy and cheap!

I'm not saying you can't or shouldn't dedicate a room to homeschooling. You definitely can; many do and enjoy it! But before spending a lot of money on a dedicated space, I'd do a few trial runs and see which area you and your children like best.

7. Transport.

If your kiddo is giving you a LOT of resistance to learning, a simple trick we like to employ is "transporting." We will transport the school outside, to a coffee shop, to a friend's home, or other places. Sometimes a change of scenery is just what everyone needs. Even a new area of the house can help. I sometimes ask, "Should we read in bed!? Can we build a fort for math worksheets?" Because you're home, you have the ability to do this. Plus, it's free and can really add vitality to your routine.

8. Currency.

If your child has a formal curriculum that they must follow, you might find your them resisting the work. This is normal. Think about your own life. If you were told that you must go to work every day and complete certain tasks, but you weren't getting paid or rewarded for it in any obvious way, what would your attitude be? Your supervisors might be able to force your compliance with threats, but you're not going to be happy about it.

But when you are working at something where you do get paid, you have more motivation to get yourself up every morning and generally try to do your job well so you don't get fired! There is no reason to think about school any differently. I'm not saying you have to pay your kids with cash, but you can try to find a currency that is valuable to them and use it to motivate. Things like screen time, video games, friend time, stickers, craft supplies, and puzzles are all good motivators.

Personally, I don't punish for noncompliance. But I do stick to not allowing them the rewards if they didn't complete the tasks. Same as if an adult doesn't get paid if they don't go to work! There are about one thousand exceptions to this rule, though, and you should absolutely be flexible and make it your own.

If your child is still putting up major resistance, you need to talk to them. Is it too hard? Too easy? Do they have attention issues? Do they not trust you? Are they picking up on your anxiety or irritation? All of these are issues for the parent to work through; this is not the child's responsibility to muscle through. If you don't find a way to solve these problems, you're likely going to be butting heads daily and it's going to be very difficult to maintain peace in the home.

In conclusion, it's important to not force learning in the home to look like traditional school. Take your child's personality, learning styles and any special needs they have into account and utilize this knowledge to your benefit. Take advantage of all the unique benefits that the home environment offers. Be kind to yourself as you work through this process and remember that trial and error is your friend here.

Chapter 19: How To Motivate Your Homeschooled Child

Motivating your children can be one of your challenges when it comes to homeschooling. When it is time for them to work on their "school stuff", it is common to hear your children complain and be less enthusiastic. You will then have to look for ways to turn learning time into a cooperative experience for you and the kids. In order for you to do so, you need to first evaluate some of your fundamental assumptions about studying.

In a traditional school environment, all students are required to learn the same things at the same rate, regardless of their abilities or interests. Frequent tests and examinations are done to know which students are getting the lessons and who are not. There are students who are always struggling to keep up with the class while other students are able to catch on quickly that they end up struggling with boredom. These situations lead to discipline and behavioral problems which you can avoid when you homeschool your children.

But the sad news is that a lot of parents try to re-create the same environment in traditional school at home. When you do this, you can expect your homeschooled children to have the same reactions as the schooled children. They can become tired or bored and stubborn, uncooperative and crabby. When you start experiencing this, you need to remind yourself that the issue is not with your children but with your mistaken idea that all your children should study a certain set of information at a certain grade or age.

•It will take you a lot of faith to start believing that your kids can and will, even though they don't follow standard curricula and lesson plans. Here are some effective techniques you can use in nurturing the love of learning in your home:

Do not encourage your children to be competitive. Tell them that they do not need to compete with their siblings or with other children to be the best student or to receive the highest grade. Teach them about real education which is not about finishing first or getting the highest grade. It is about learning how to love the act of learning. Teach your children to focus on the learning process instead of the outcome.

•Avoid comparing your kids to other children. It does not really matter whether your neighbor's 5-year-old is already writing script or your friend's 6-year-old can already recite the multiplication table. Give your children the freedom to learn when they are ready to learn.

•Do not encourage rote memorization. Keep in mind that your children will eventually forget 80% of the information they have memorized during the previous year. Children, and even adults, remember only the things that they are interested in.

If you allow your children to pursue their interests and passions, they will learn a lot without much effort.

•Do not get into the habit of promising rewards for academic achievements. Do not give your children the wrong reasons to be motivated because it will only be temporary. Instead of becoming a truly self-motivated learner, your children will get used to getting the reward as their goal. Research studies have revealed that rewards can basically result to dislike of or apathy for the rewarded subject which totally negates your original objective.

•Do not put the blame on your children when things are not going well with your efforts to homeschool them. Instead of blaming yourself or your children, it is better to start stepping back. Take a break in order to better see what you have been doing and look for better ways to do your tasks. You can also start talking with other parents who homeschool their kids to ask for tips or advice. Read more resources to find out better techniques to help your children. You need to be flexible enough to change your approach and try something new.

•Make your home "education friendly". Give your children easy access to learning tools and resources such as interesting books, arts and crafts supplies, science equipment (magnets, thermometers, scales), magazines and catalogs, musical instruments and music books, writing and office supplies, math manipulatives and calculators, maps and a globe and a microscope or telescope.

•When your children are doing their homeschool activities, make sure that the TV is turned off. Do not allow them to play in their Game Boy, smartphone or tablet.

•Go to the public library on a regular basis so you and your children can check out different books on interesting new topics.

•Gear your lessons towards the interests of your children. Look for topics that inspire them and do not hesitate to follow their lead. You can study geometry by building a birdhouse, horticulture by gardening, fractions by baking and science using insects.

•Give your children enough space to make a mess. Provide them with a table that is reserved for their ongoing projects.

•Give your children specific guidelines as to what they are expected to do and complete every day. You can use a dry-erase board to do this. This will allow your children to focus their attention on what needs to be done before they play and do other tasks.

•Don't be too hard on your children when they reach a down time and they are not generating much output. During this slow period, simply support and encourage them. It is typically followed by an intellectual growth spurt so you just need to be patient.

- Be a good example to your children. If you want them to read more, show them how much you love to read. Write them letters. Play educational games with them. Show them that you also look up things that you don't know. Show them that you have the willingness to learn a new task or try an unfamiliar activity. Your children will mirror what they see at home. You can expect your kids to be hooked on the television if they always see you spending your free time in front of the television.

Be your children's learning partner. You can view homeschooling as a great way for you to study all the wonderful things that you missed when you were going to school. You can view yourself as a facilitator who guides, provides learning opportunities and creates an atmosphere where your children can learn as part of their day to day lifestyle than something that only happen during "school time".

Chapter 20: How To Find Programs For Homeschooled Kids' Social Interaction

Once you decide to teach your children at home, you must also decide what kind of homeschooling program you will use. There are many homeschooling programs to choose from, and your choice will determine how you teach your children. Among other things, you must also consider if you want an accredited home school program. An accredited program will make it easier for your child to transition into college or a public school.

You have to determine the reason for teaching your children at home instead of a regular public or private school. You may want to home school your children for religious reasons, or to give them a more well-rounded education. Your children may be gifted and bored at a regular school, or they may be lagging behind in their schoolwork and needing one-on-one attention. Once you have identified the reason, you can start looking for the right program.

Keep in mind that with home schooling you will be teaching your own children. Assess your abilities honestly and determine if you are capable of teaching all the different subjects required for a homeschooling program. If you are weak in certain areas, you must find a program that will supplement your abilities.

Although many programs are now available, not all programs have the right balance of structure and simplicity in the curriculum that you may want. This can make it difficult to decide on the right type of program.

There are many different types of home schooling programs, including online interactive courses and videos. Some programs include grade record sheets, weekly lesson plans, attendance log, and reading list forms. Some even include awards and certificates. An effective program should contain a combination of traditional education as well as unstructured learning activities such as field trips.

You may also want to consider integrating certain values in the homeschooling curriculum. There are many programs based on the Christian faith that contain teachings from the Bible. Other programs stress humanist or non-religious issues. Chances are you can probably find a program that covers your designated faith.

When choosing a program for teaching your children at home, try to find one that inculcates the values you want your children to learn. Once you find a suitable program, you can use it for your children's educational needs.

Should you opt for an accredited home school program, it will still be possible to include lessons on values or faith. Homeschooling programs are flexible, allowing you to incorporate special life lessons into the curriculum.

You can purchase pre-packaged curriculum, make your own curriculum, or you could even teach a combination of both. Some parents prefer to focus their teachings on their religious beliefs. However, it is important to keep an open mind and remember that your children are their own people and they should be taught about the world from many different perspectives. Remember that there is no "right" way to teach your children because the "right" way for one child may not be "right" for another. It is important to be flexible and change your curriculum to tailor to your children as you discover their individual requirements as they grow.

So what is Pre-Packaged Curriculum anyway? Well Pre-Packaged, "school in a box", or "all-in-one" Curriculum are comprehensive education packages that cover many subjects (usually an entire year worth). They contain all required books and materials. Some even include pencils and writing paper. The intent of the "school in a box" is to try to recreate the school environment in the home.

They are typically based on the same subject-area expectations as public schools, which allows an easy transition into school after being home schooled, if desired. They are among the most expensive options for the homeschooled, but are easy to use and require minimal preparation.

The majority of today's home-educated students use an eclectic mix of materials for their Homeschooling needs. For example, they might use a pre-designed program for language, arts or mathematics, and fill in history with reading and field trips, art with classes at a community center, science through home school science clubs, physical education with memberships in local sports teams, etc. This has been proven to be one of the most successful ways of educating the Homeschooled child.

Home educators are also able to take advantage of educational programs at museums, community centers, athletic clubs, after-school programs, churches, science preserves, parks, and other community resources. Secondary school level students often take classes at community colleges, which typically have open admission policies.

One of the major benefits of Homeschooling is the ability to blend lessons using a central theme, for example, a study unit about Native Americans could combine lessons in: social studies - like how different tribes live now and lived prior to colonization; art - such as making Native American clothing;

history of Native Americans in the US; reading from a specialized reading list; and the science of plants used by Native Americans. You could use this same technique on another study unit where you chose another broad topic to study.

Homeschooling also offers student paced learning. This is similar to "all-in-one" curriculum and is often referred to as "Paces". These workbooks allow the student to progress at an appropriate speed that suits their individual needs. They allow the student to master concepts, before moving on to the next subject, instead relying on the speed of the teacher and other students where they may move on to the next subject too quickly or not move on quickly enough.

Another form of Homeschooling is "Unschooling", that is, an area in which students are not directly instructed but encouraged to learn through exploring their interests. Known also as "interest-led" or "child-led" learning, Unschooling attempts to provide opportunities with games and real life problems where a child will learn without coercion.

Unschooling advocates claim that children learn best by doing. A child may learn reading and math skills by playing card games, better spelling and other writing skills because he's inspired to write a science fiction story for publication, or local history by following a zoning or historical-status dispute.

No matter which technique you decide to use when you start Homeschooling your children, you should remember to be flexible and revise your teaching choices, as you will need to adapt your curriculum to better tailor to your child's needs as they become apparent.

Conclusion

The reasons for the two subjects to decide on homeschooling are the desire to provide education based on children's talents and interests, factors distrust of formal schooling, the desire to provide religious teaching, provide education for children with special needs and health problems, and alternative educational needs that accommodate the potential of students. Homeschooling decisions as alternative learning in both homeschoolers are chosen as a form of fulfillment of children's educational needs based on each child's unique learning style. Alternative learning is driven by factors from within individual children, namely: feeling bored with formal schooling so that they want to try new things, expect learning experiences with real objects, the desire to explore nature, and feel less challenged with practical lesson .

Homeschooling is an alternative education for both homeschoolers with the implementation of learning using the curriculum from the government, but managed independently and flexibly based on children's autonomy. Homeschooler expressed satisfaction in implementing homeschooling because it can be fully responsible in designing learning based on the child's potential. other than that parents can control the learning activities of homeschooling children as well as a form of prevention of deviant behavior in children.

www.ingramcontent.com/pod-product-compliance
Lightning Source LLC
Chambersburg PA
CBHW071831080526
44589CB00012B/985